Skulls

Grown-Up Coloring Book

Over 40 Skulls to Color

One image per page

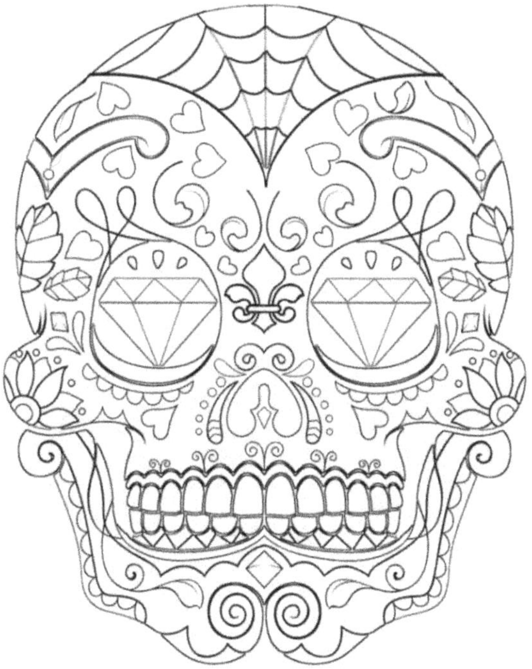

Sign up for our email list at **www.calmdalas.com**

Get notified about new books and get 5 **FREE** Skulls!

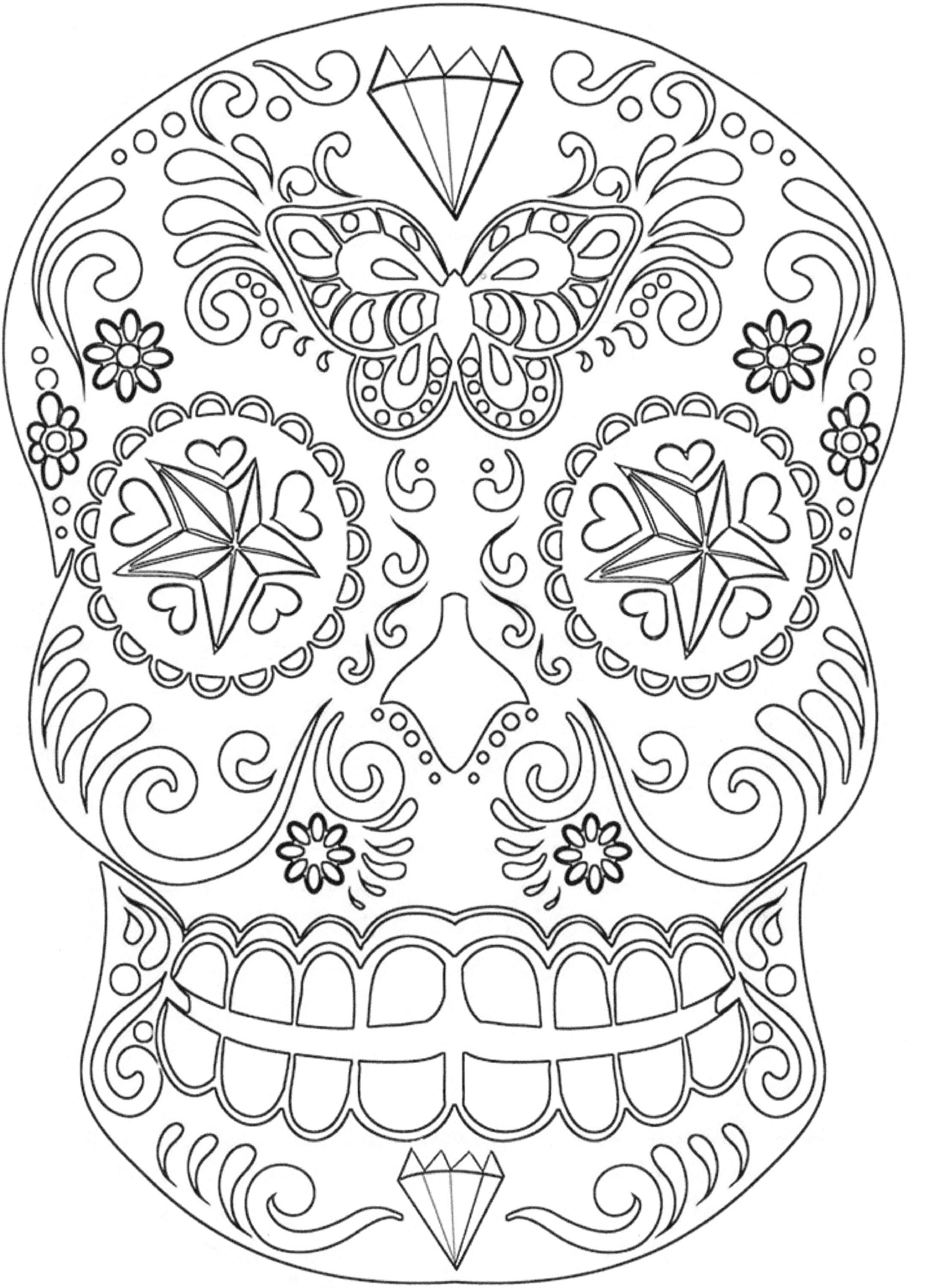

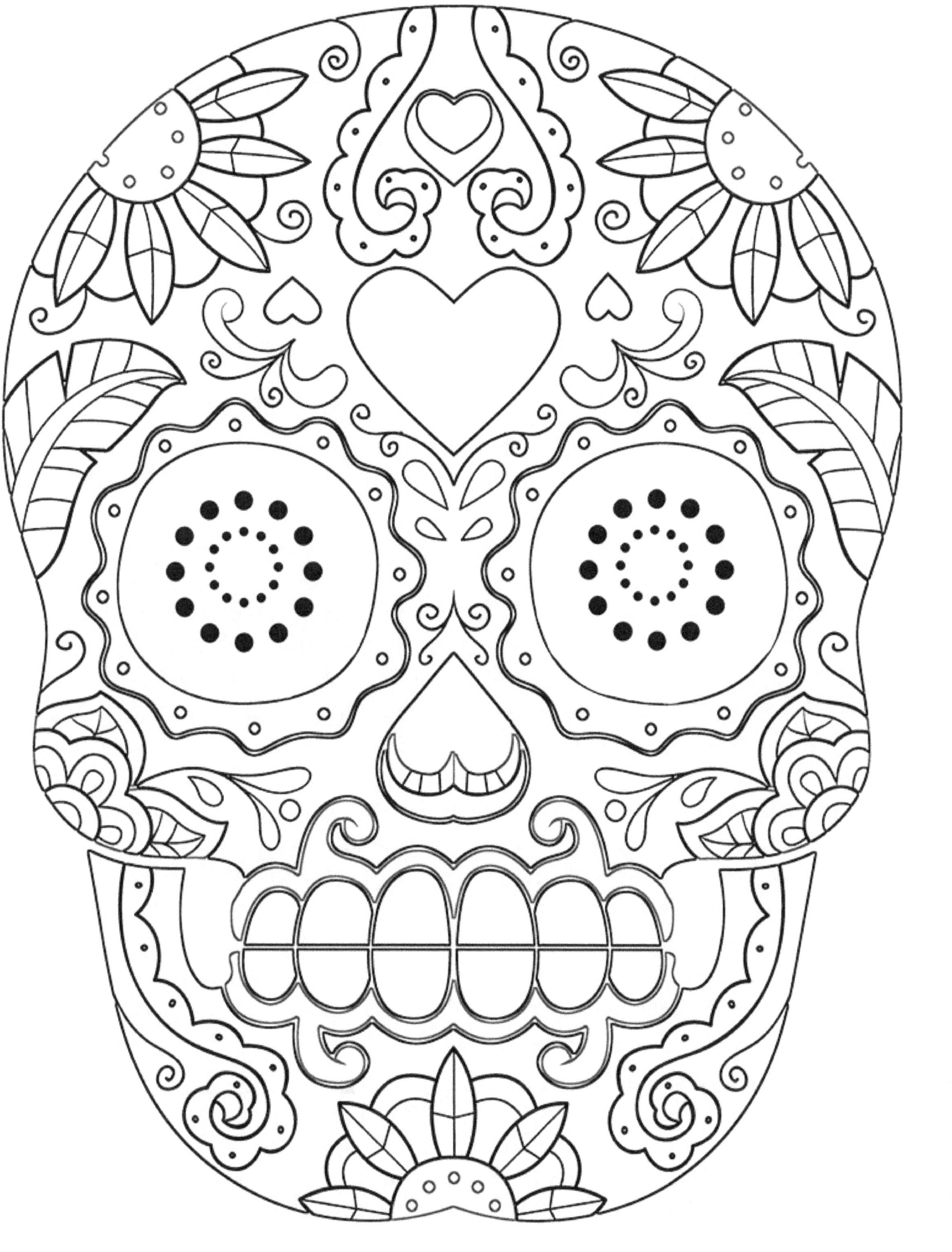

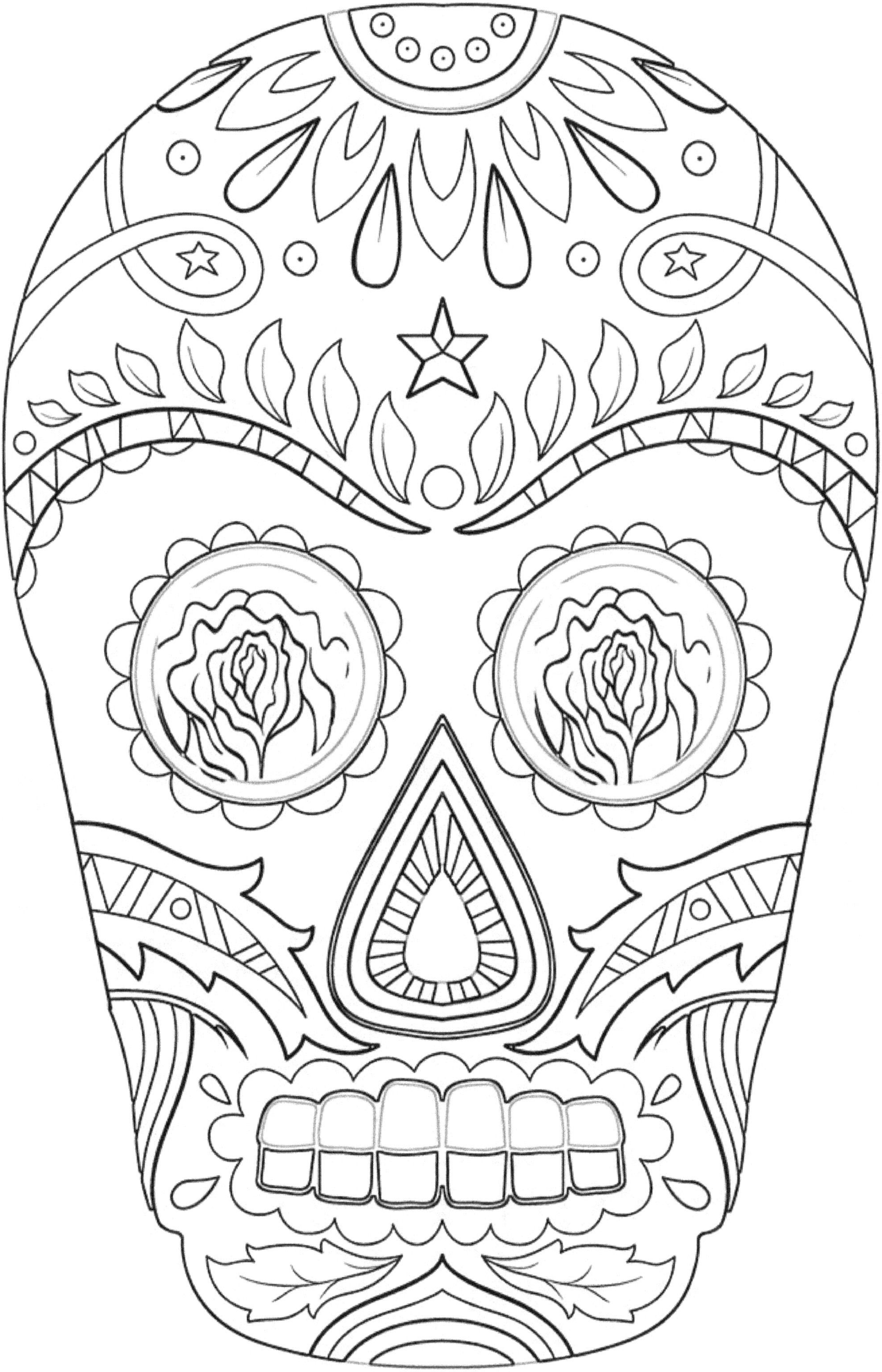

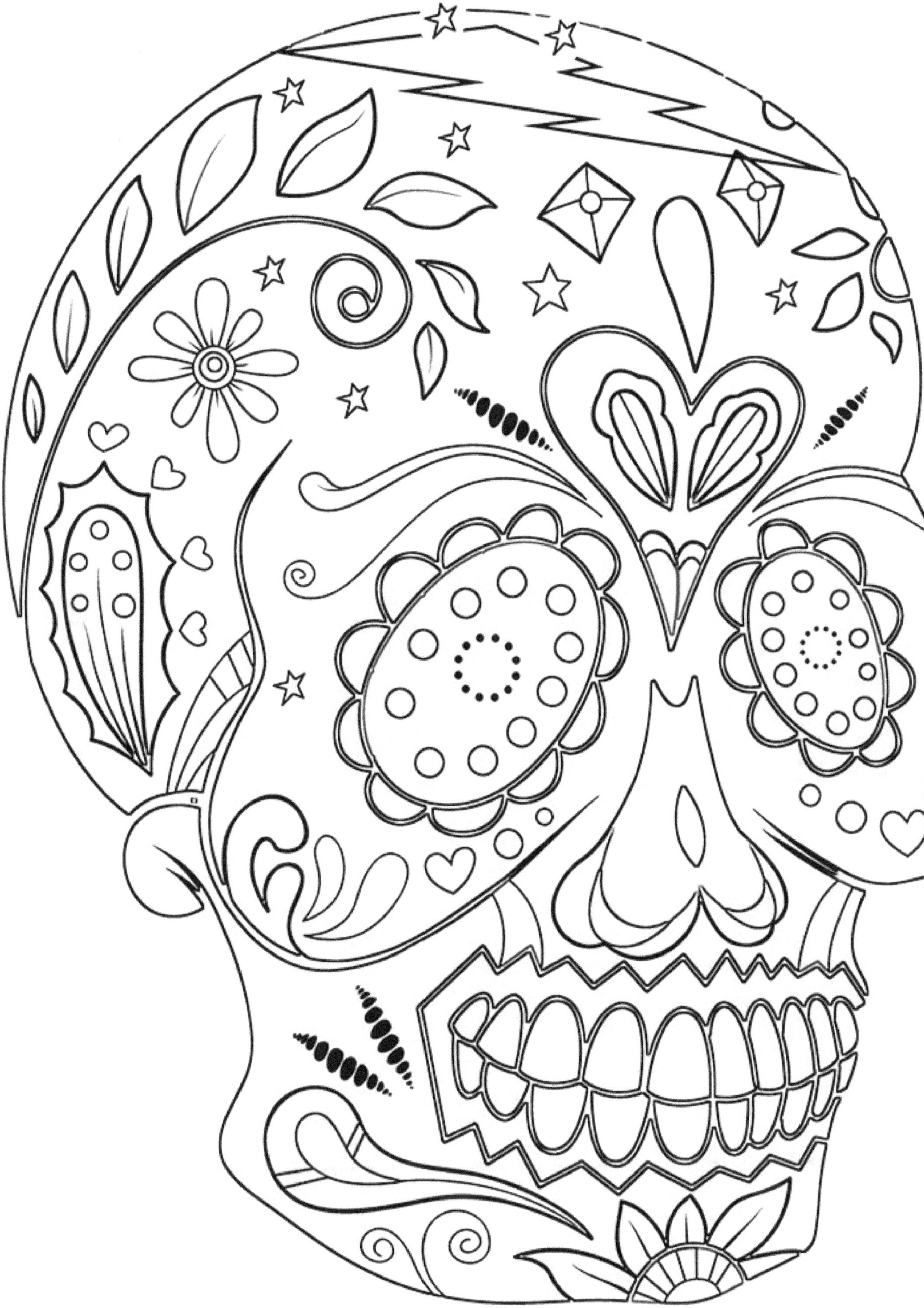

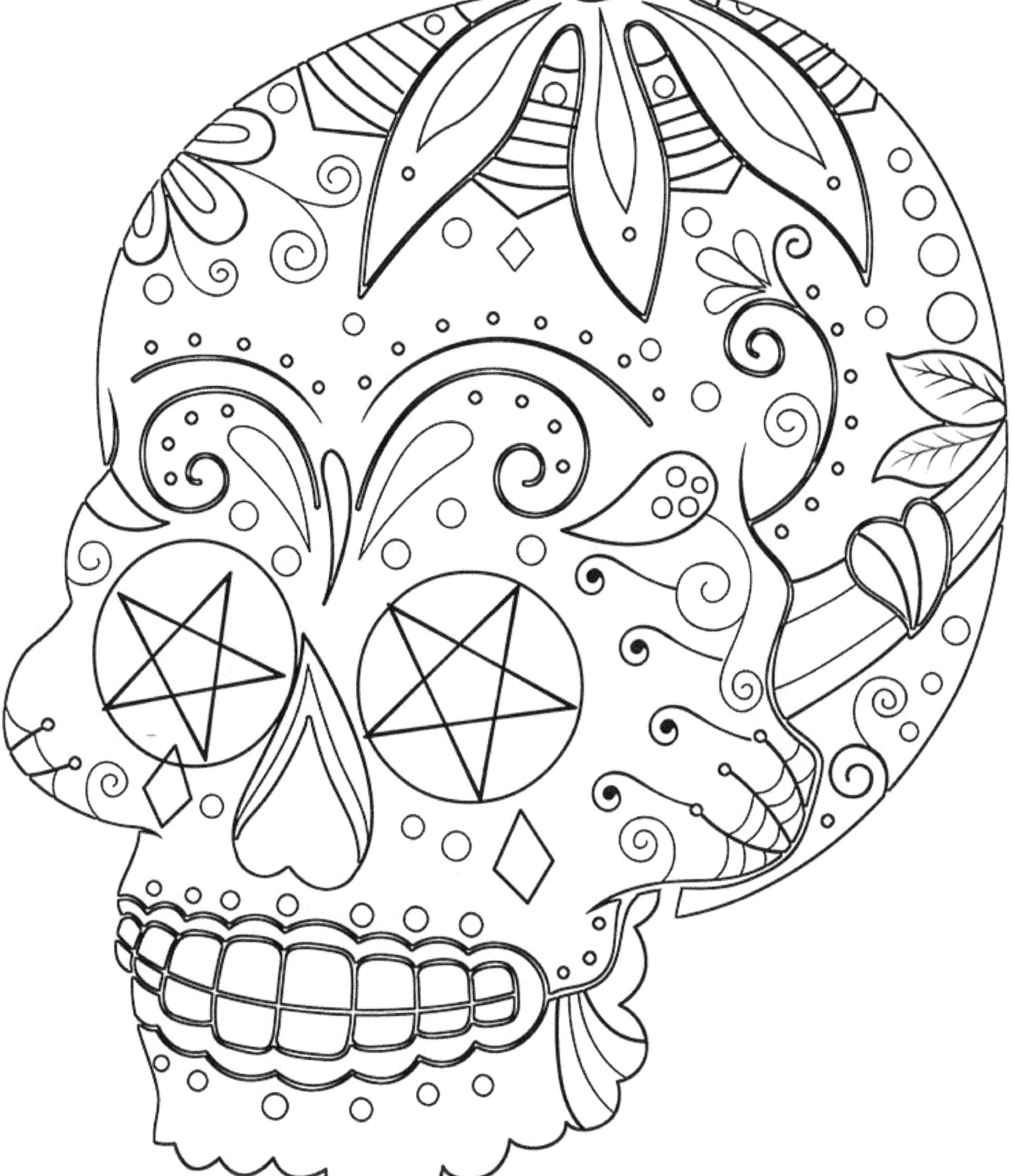

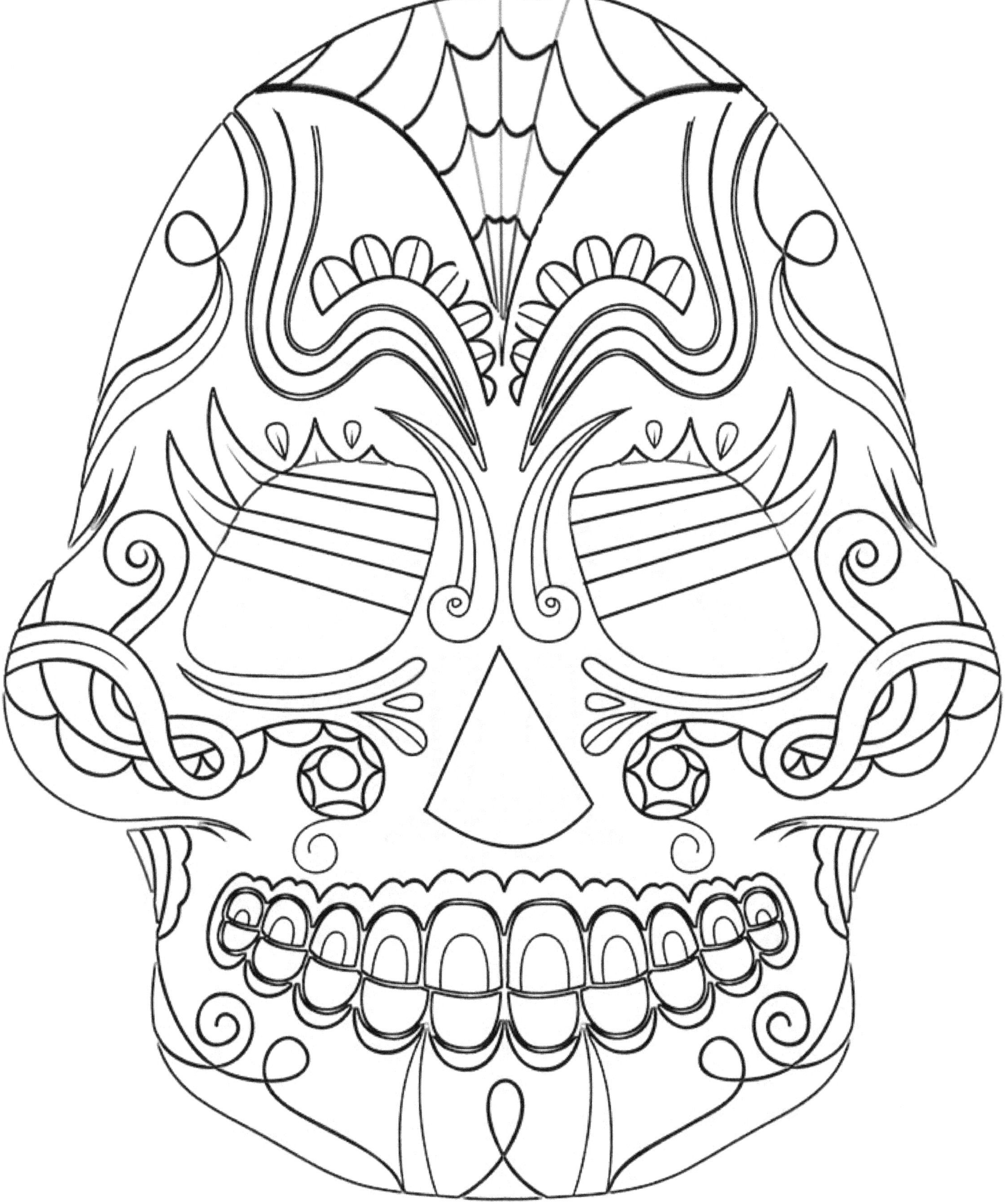

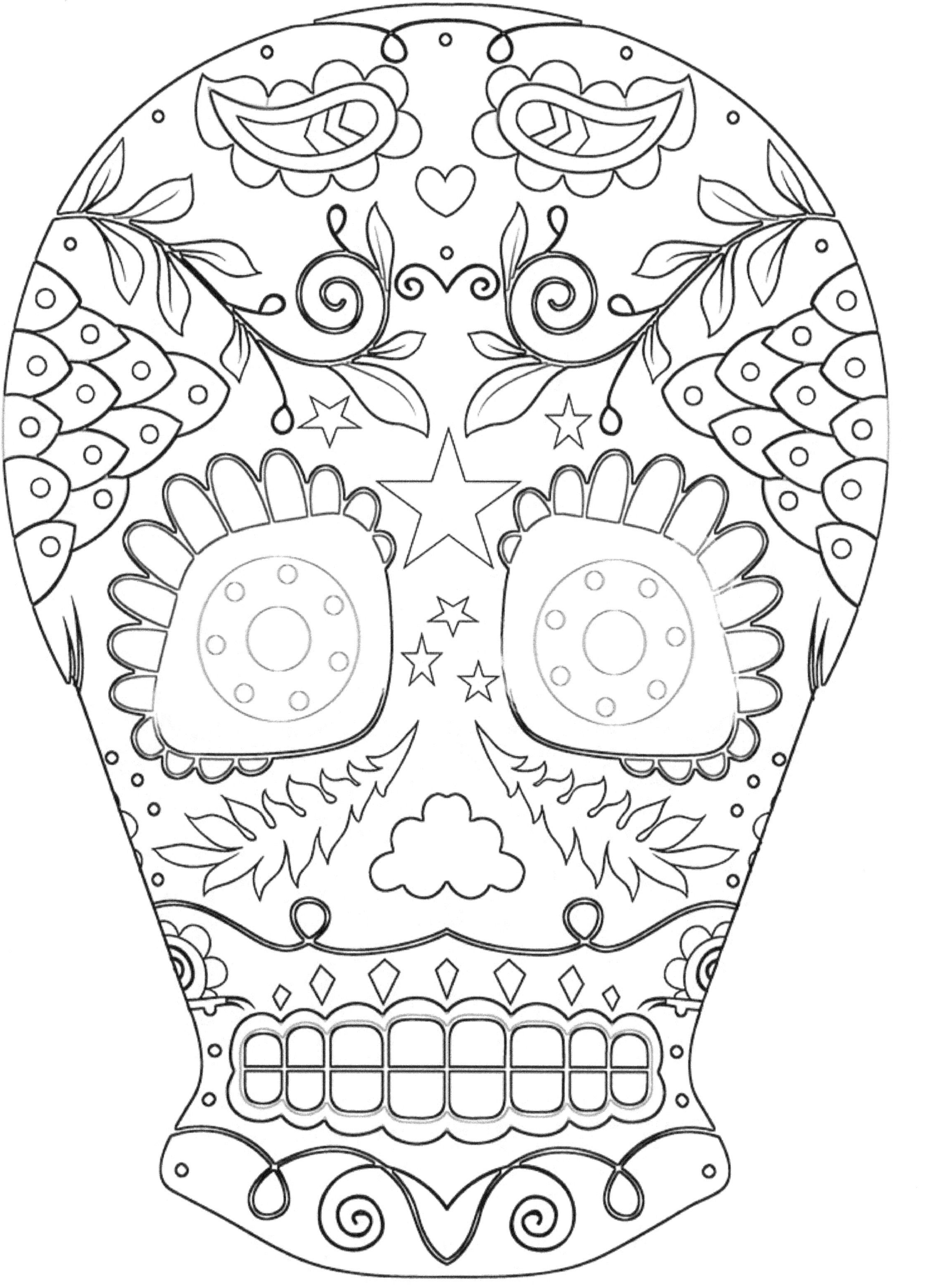

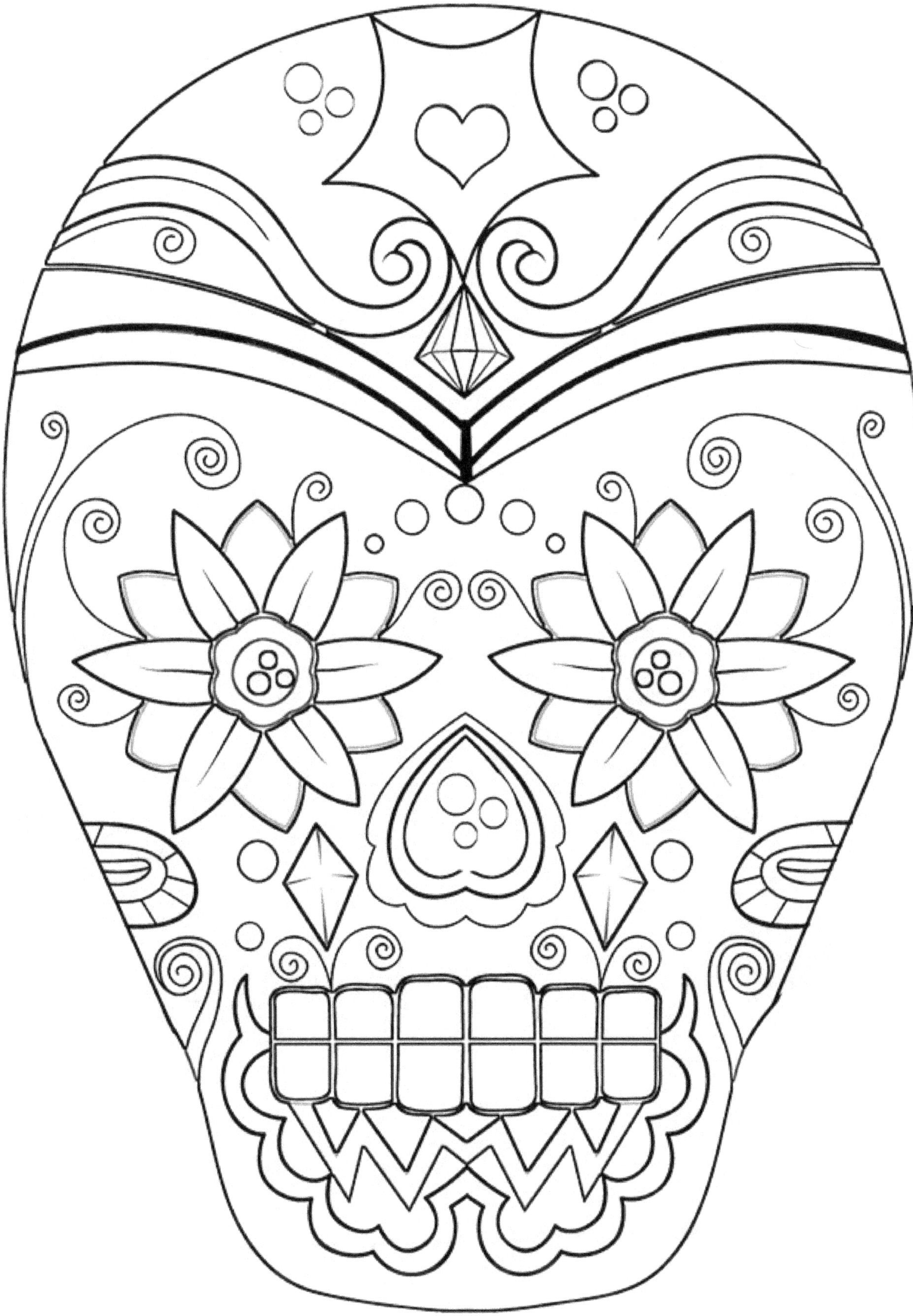

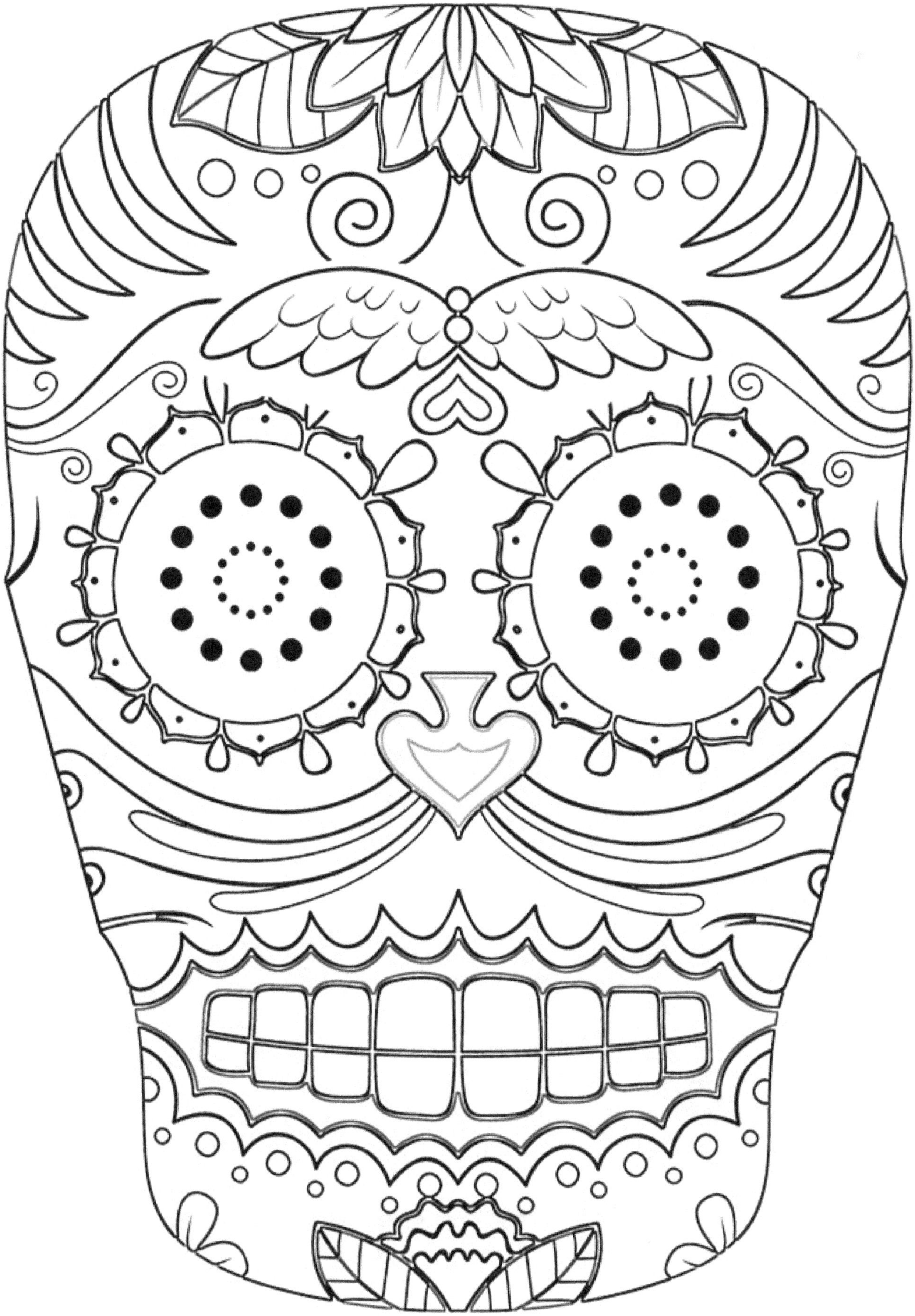

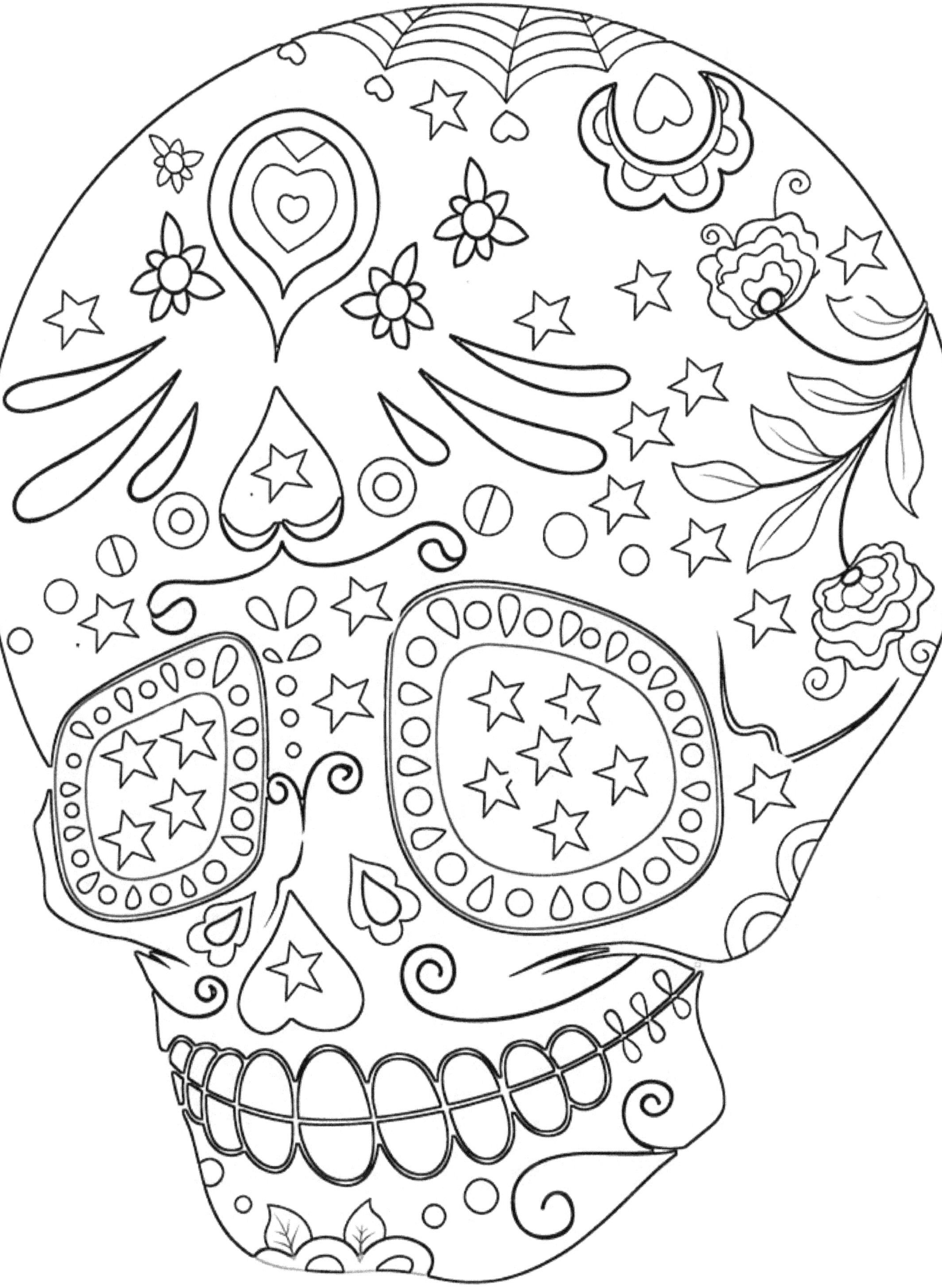

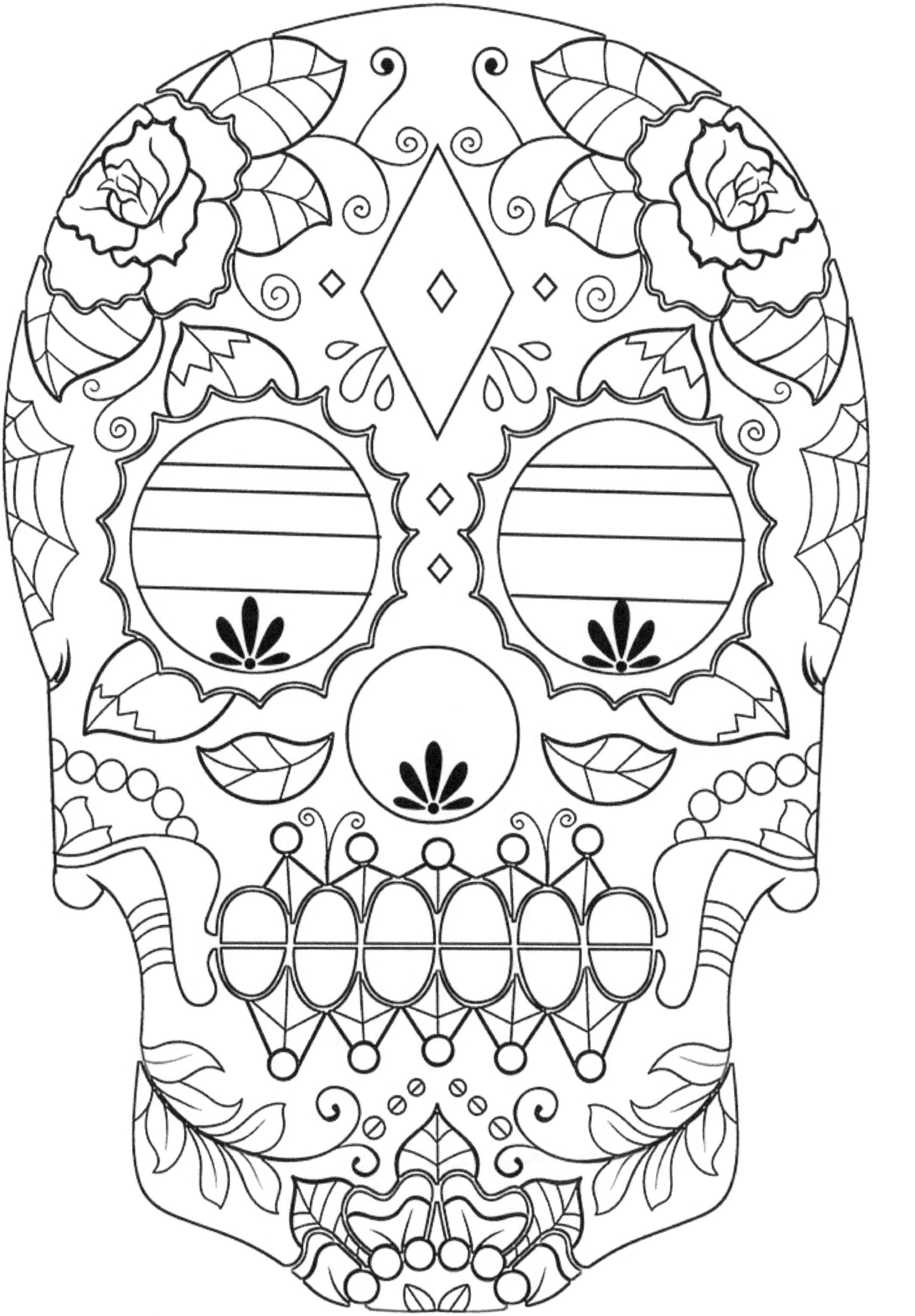

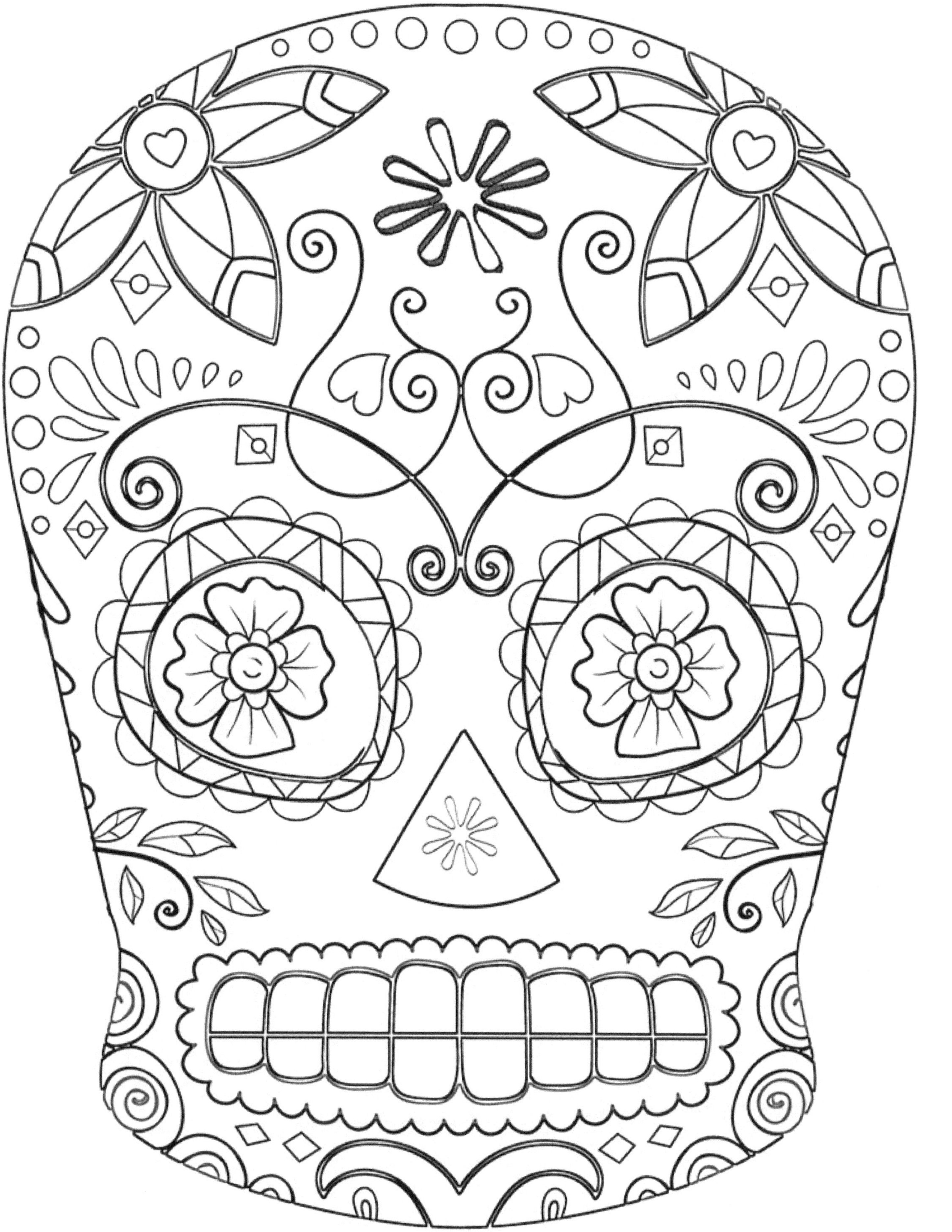

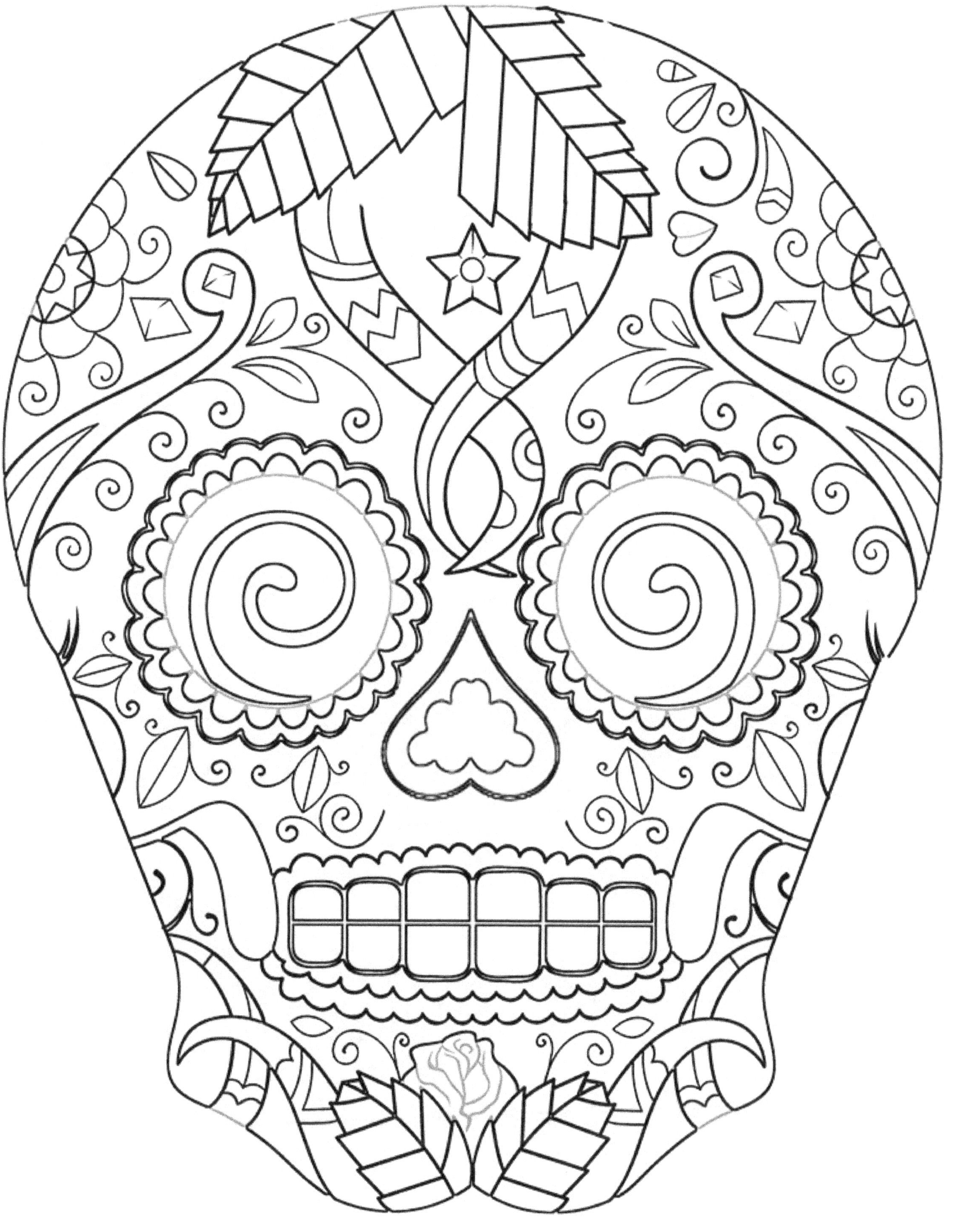

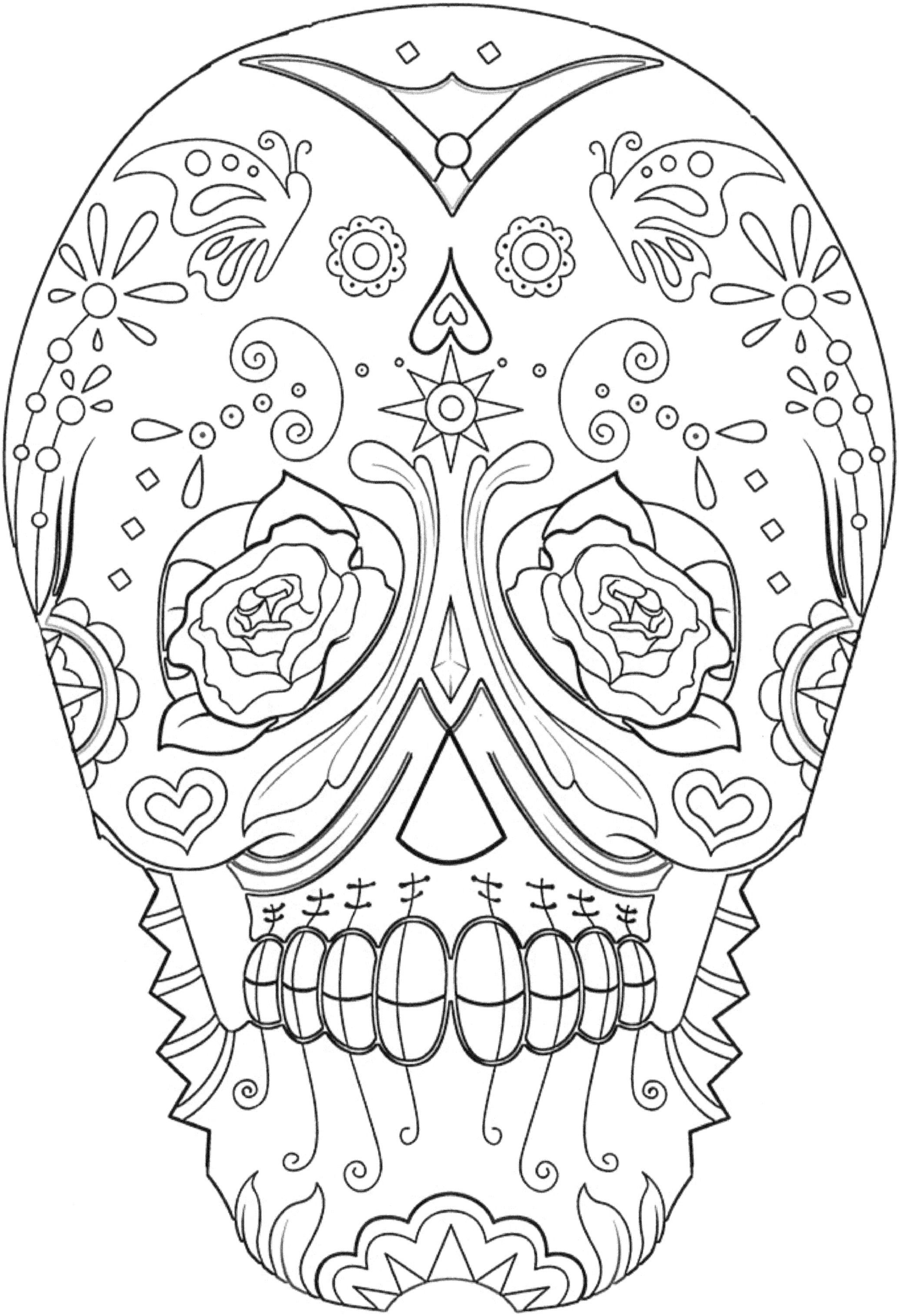

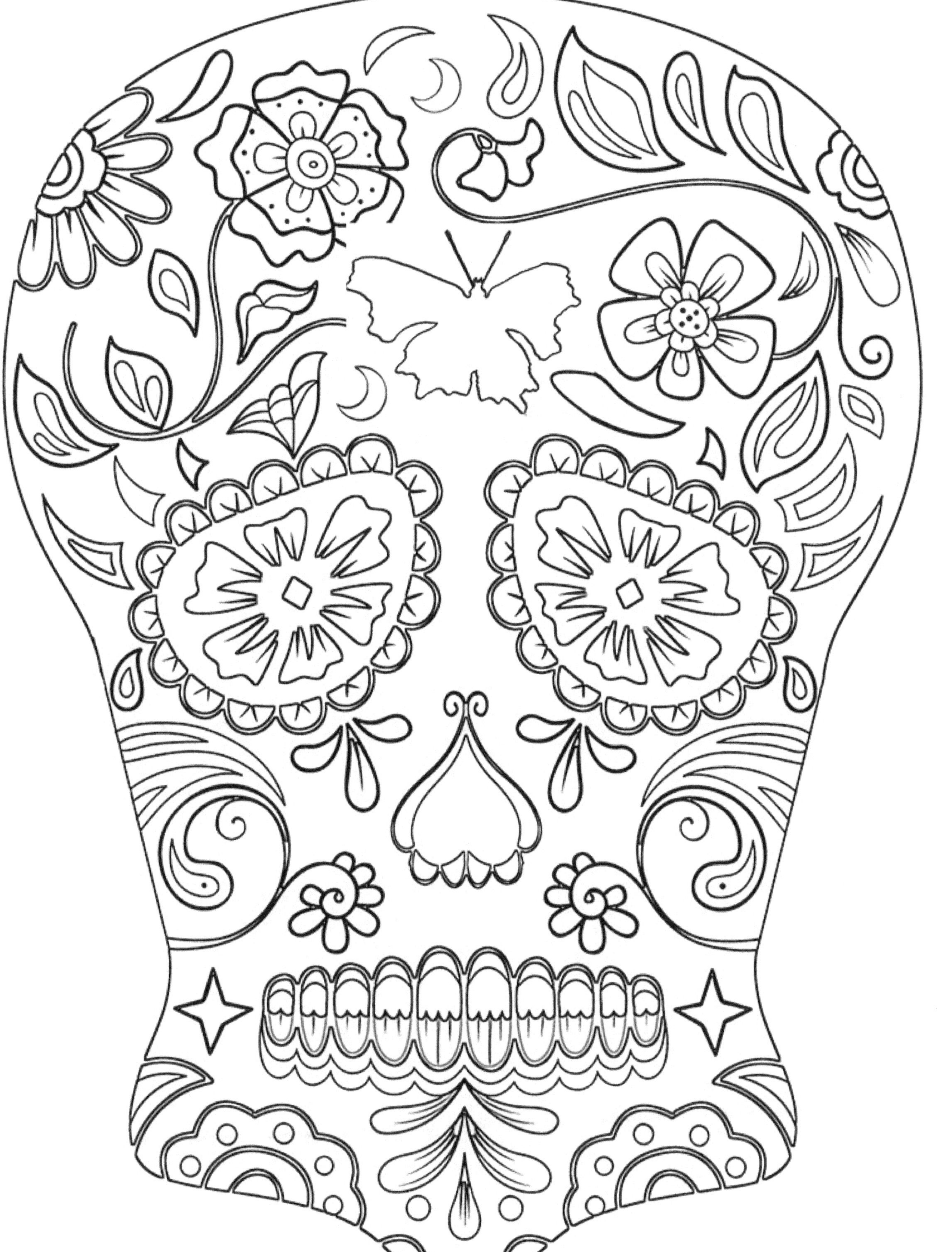

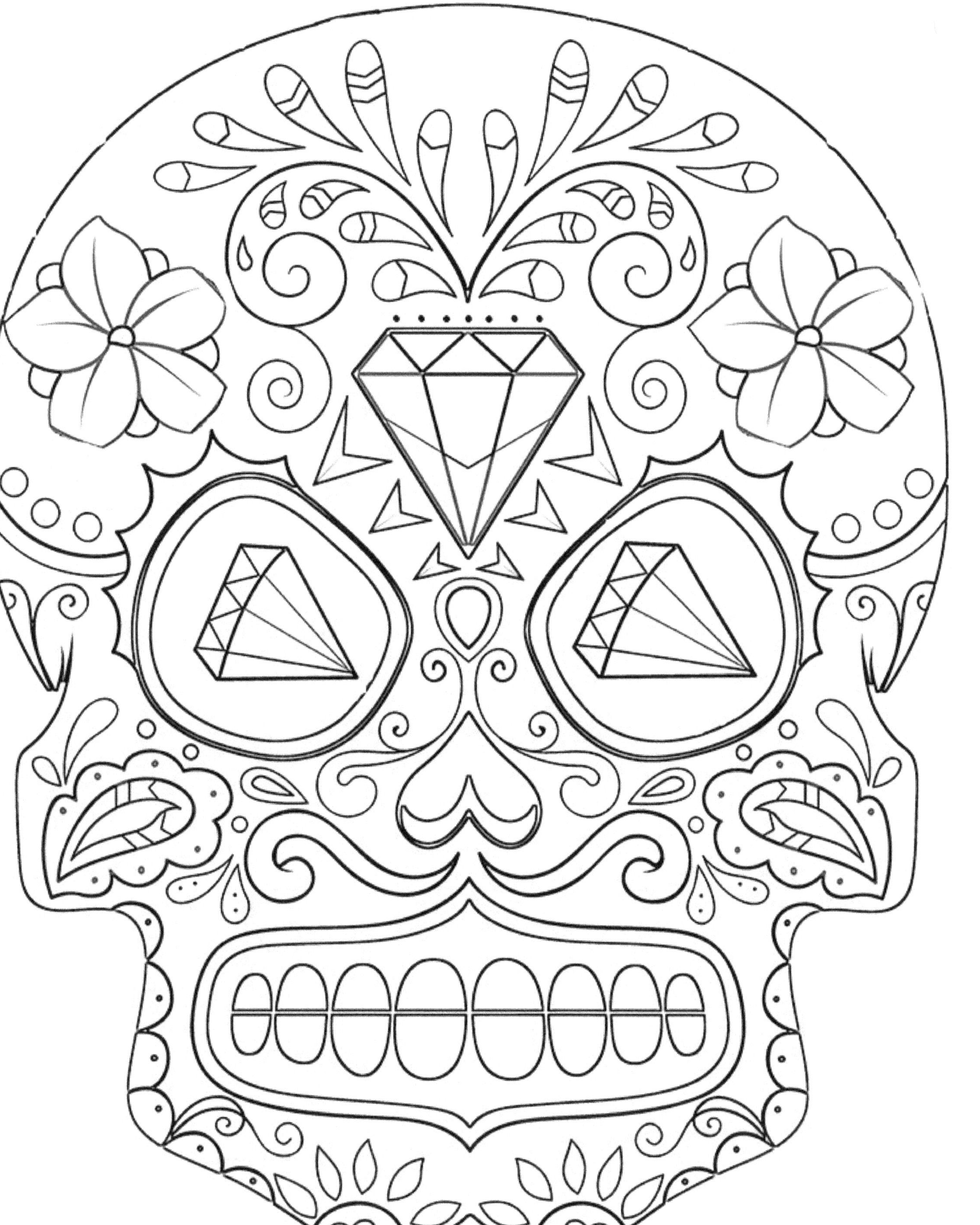

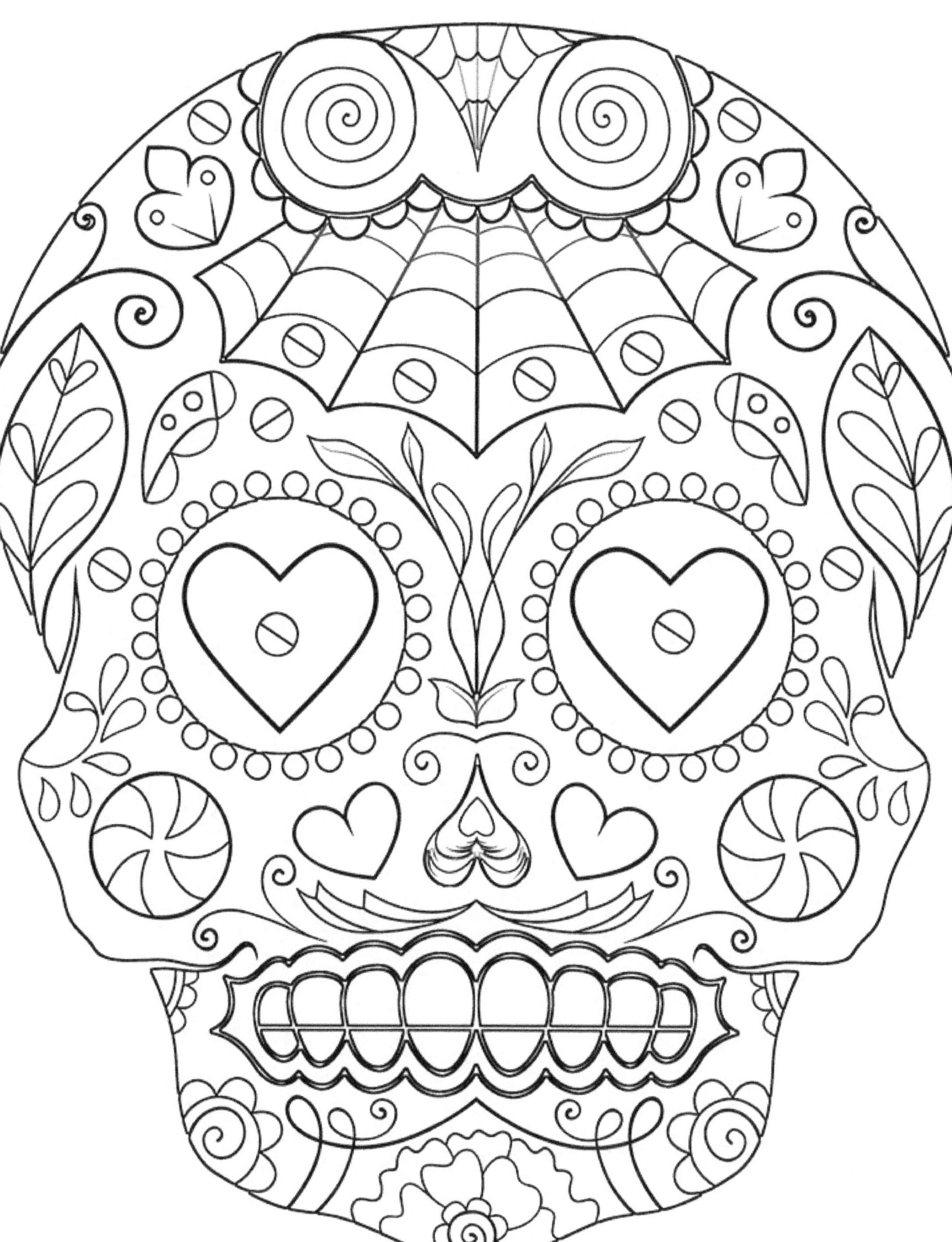

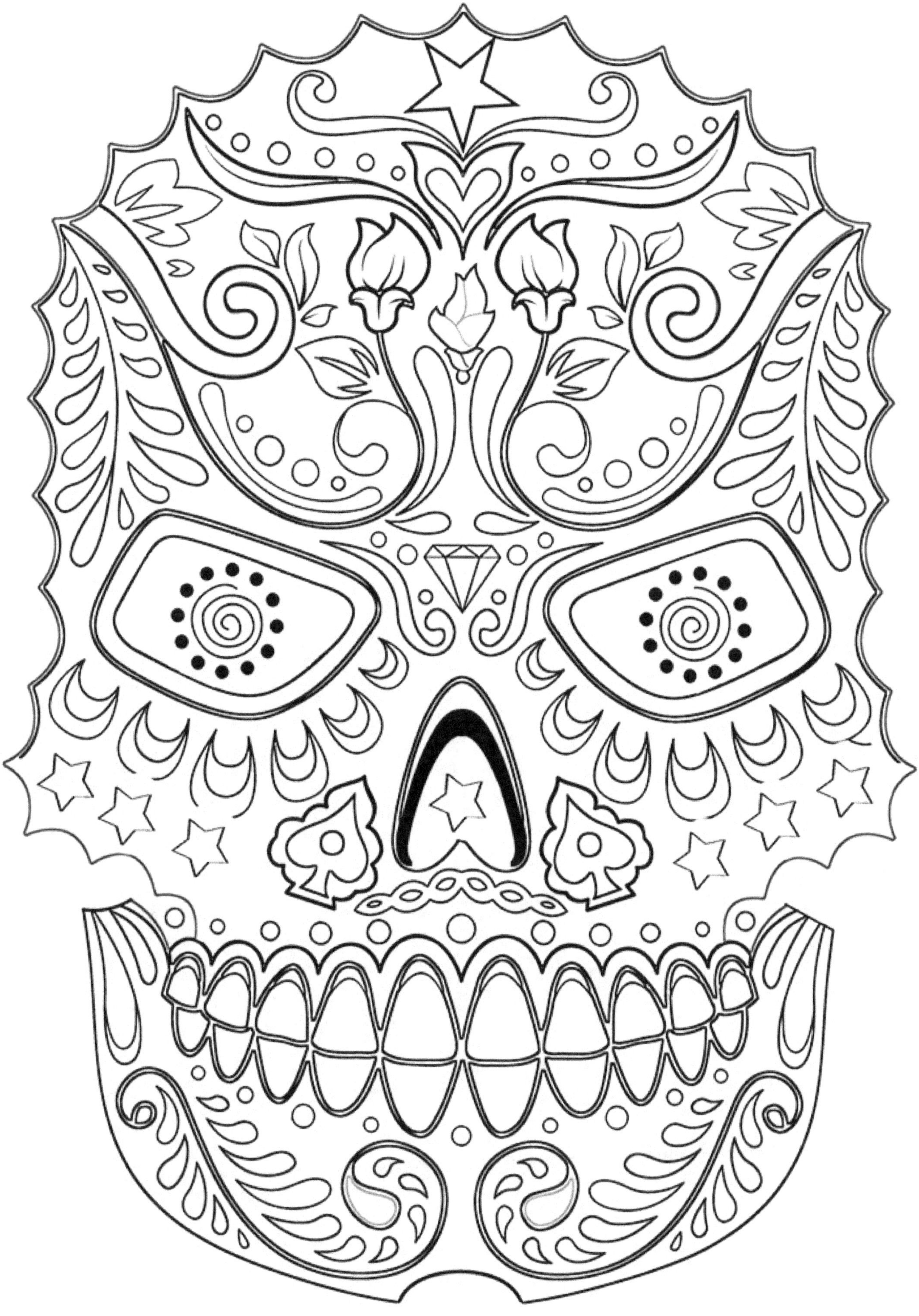

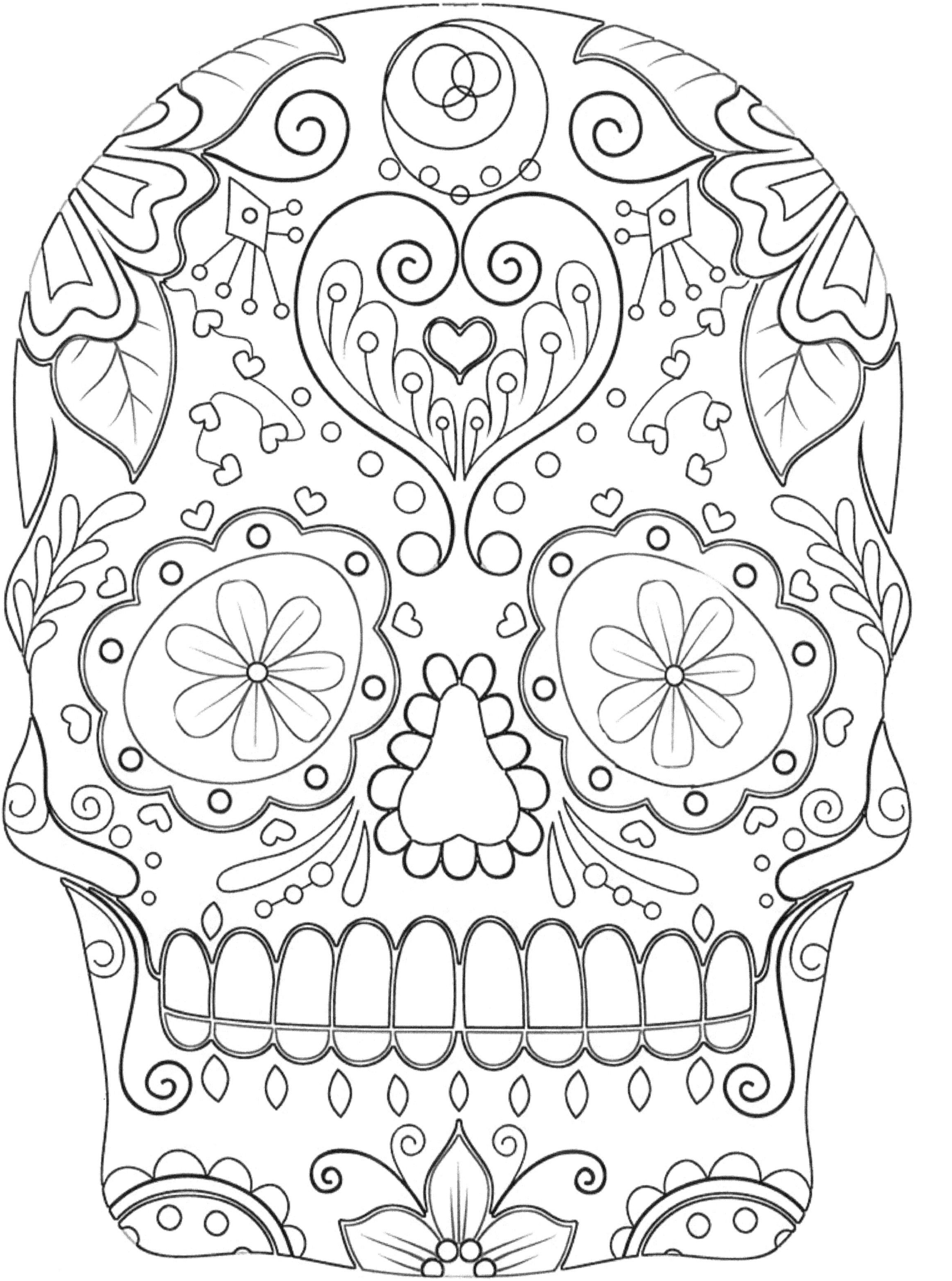

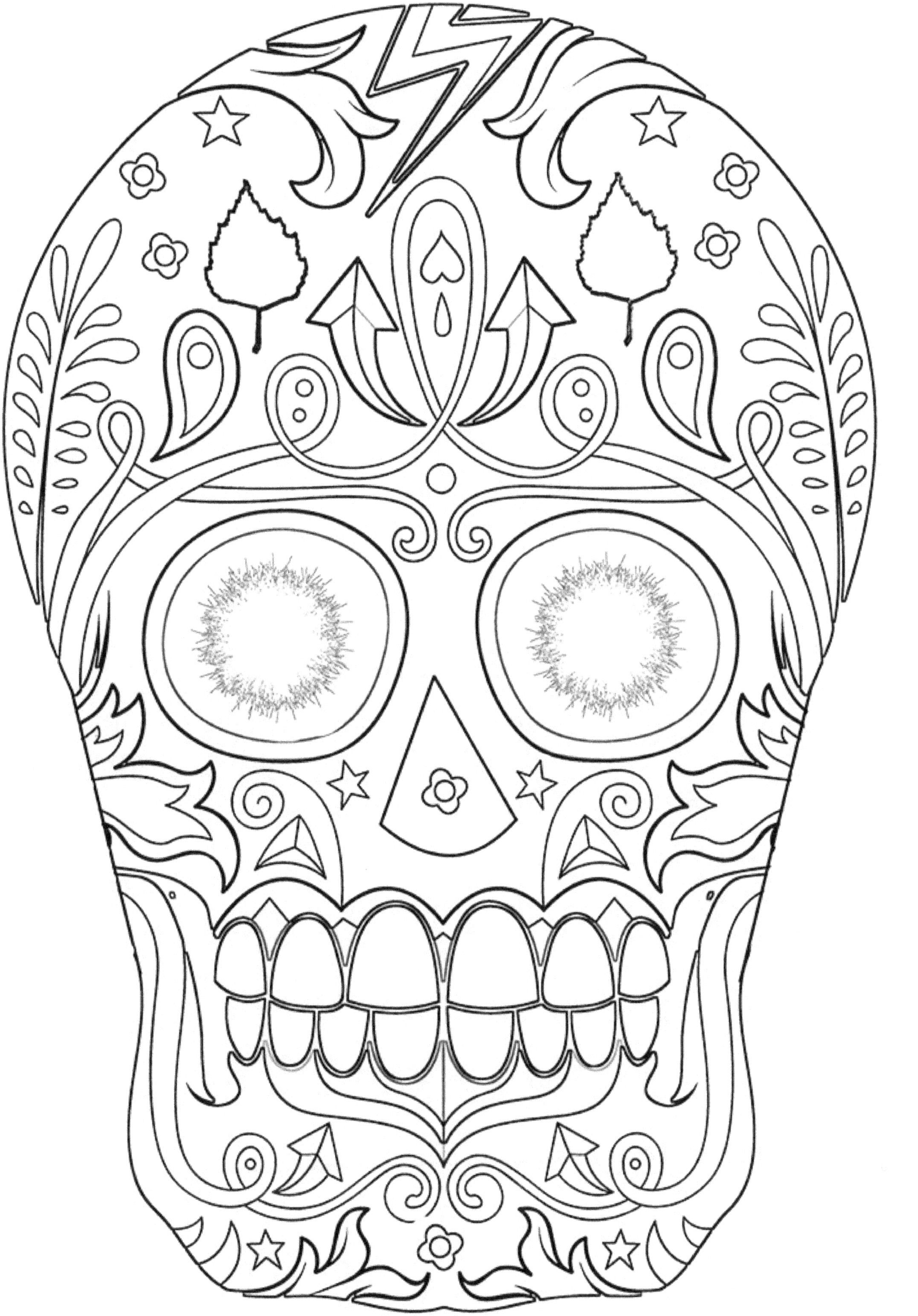

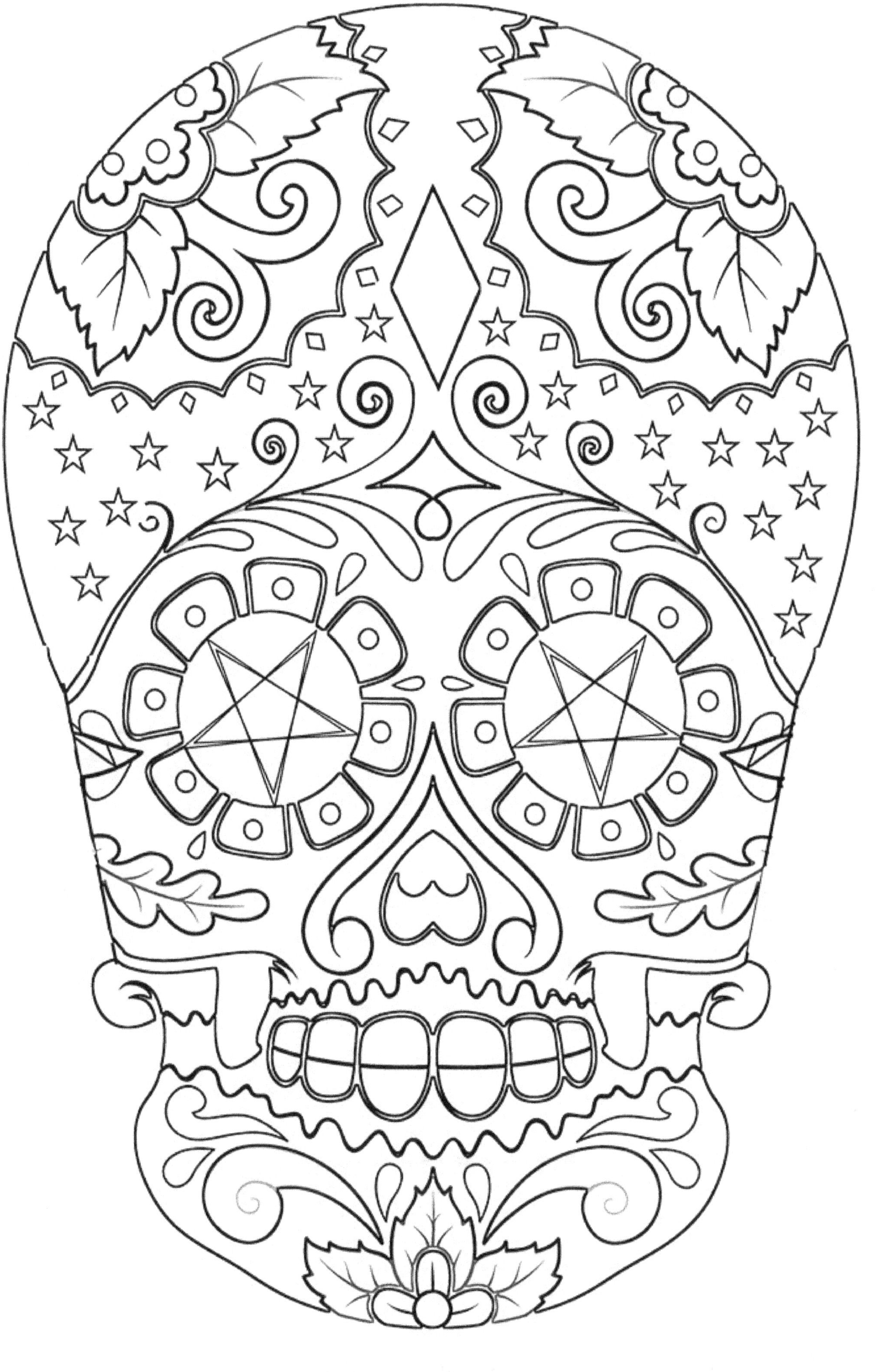

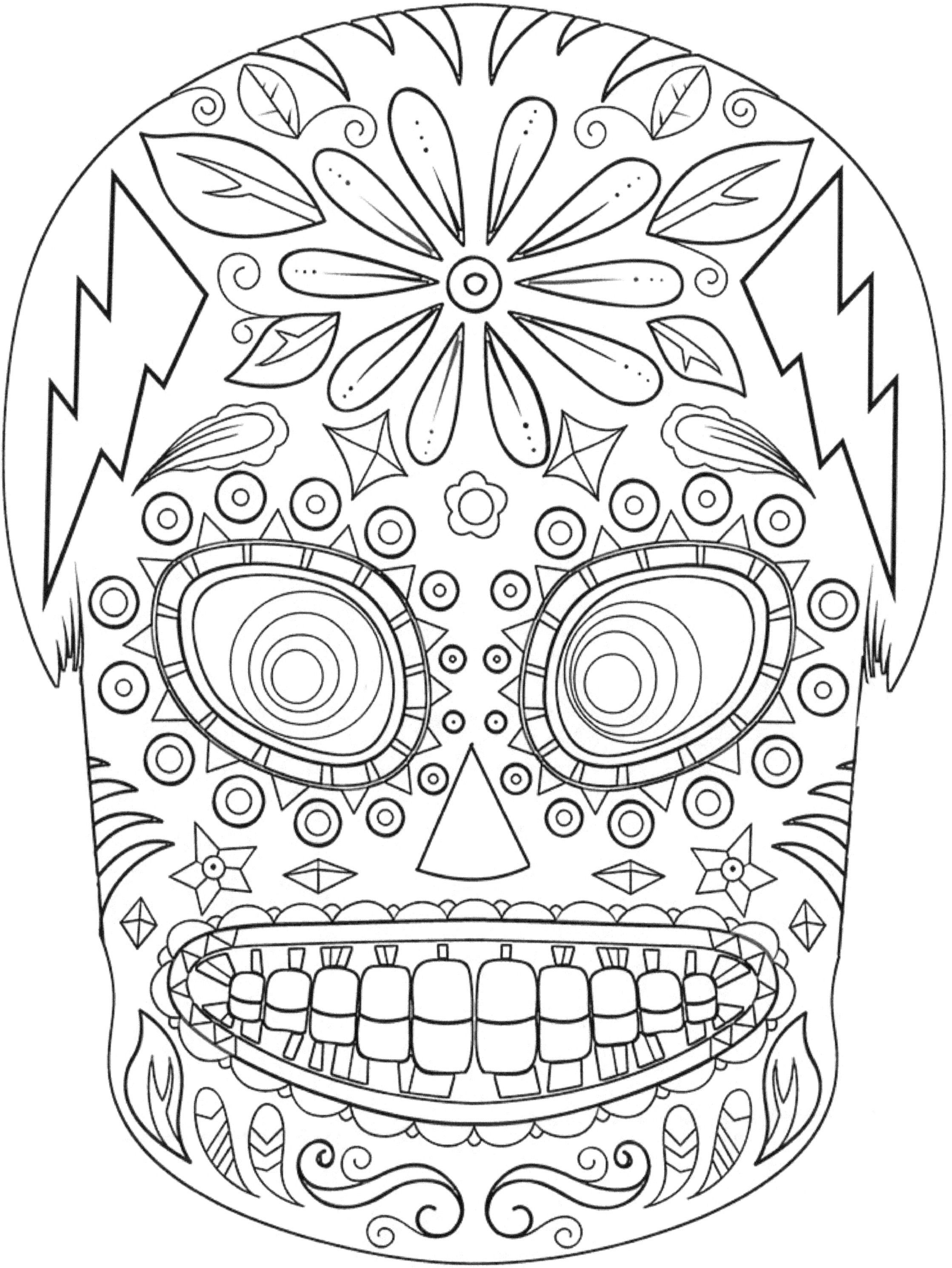

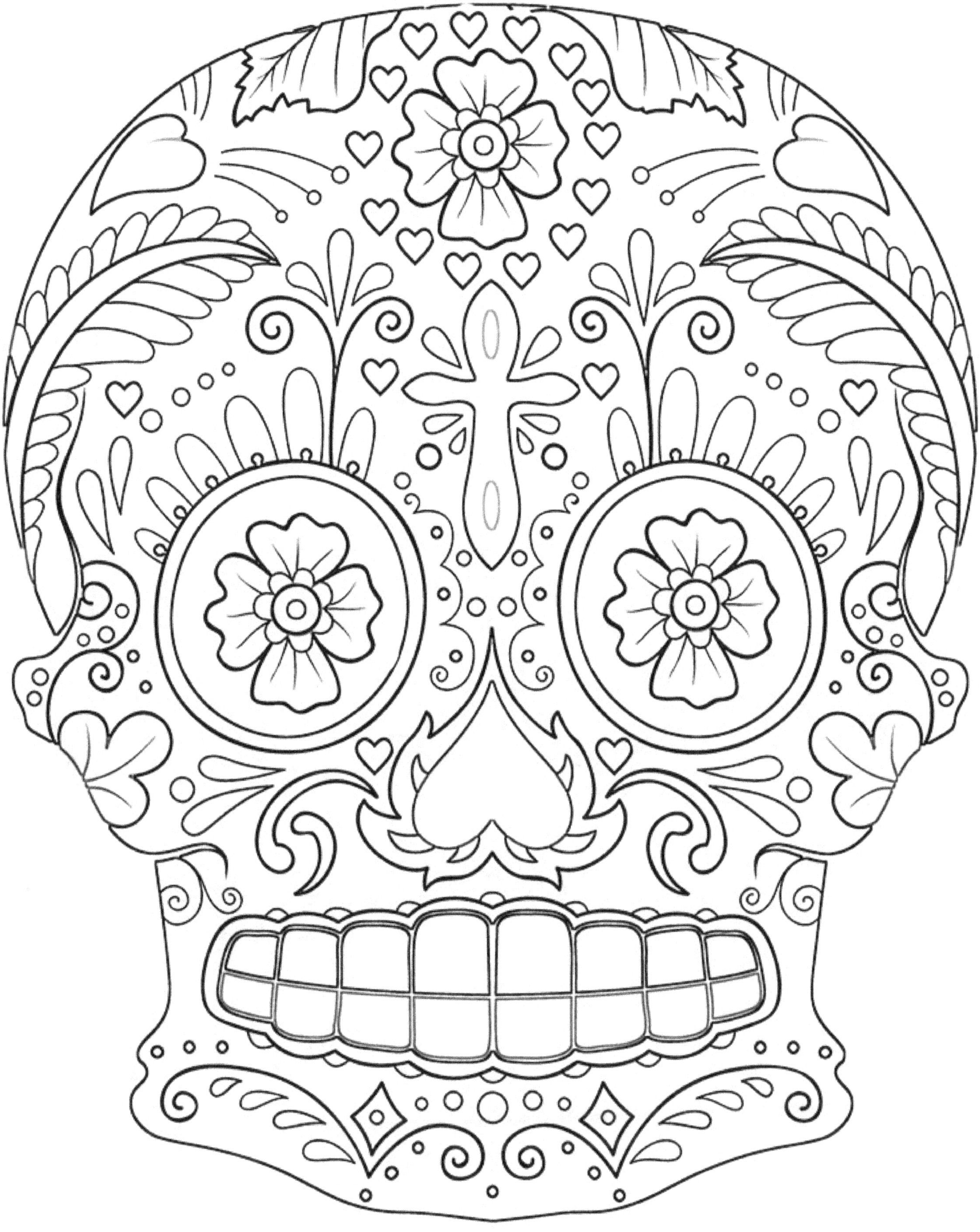

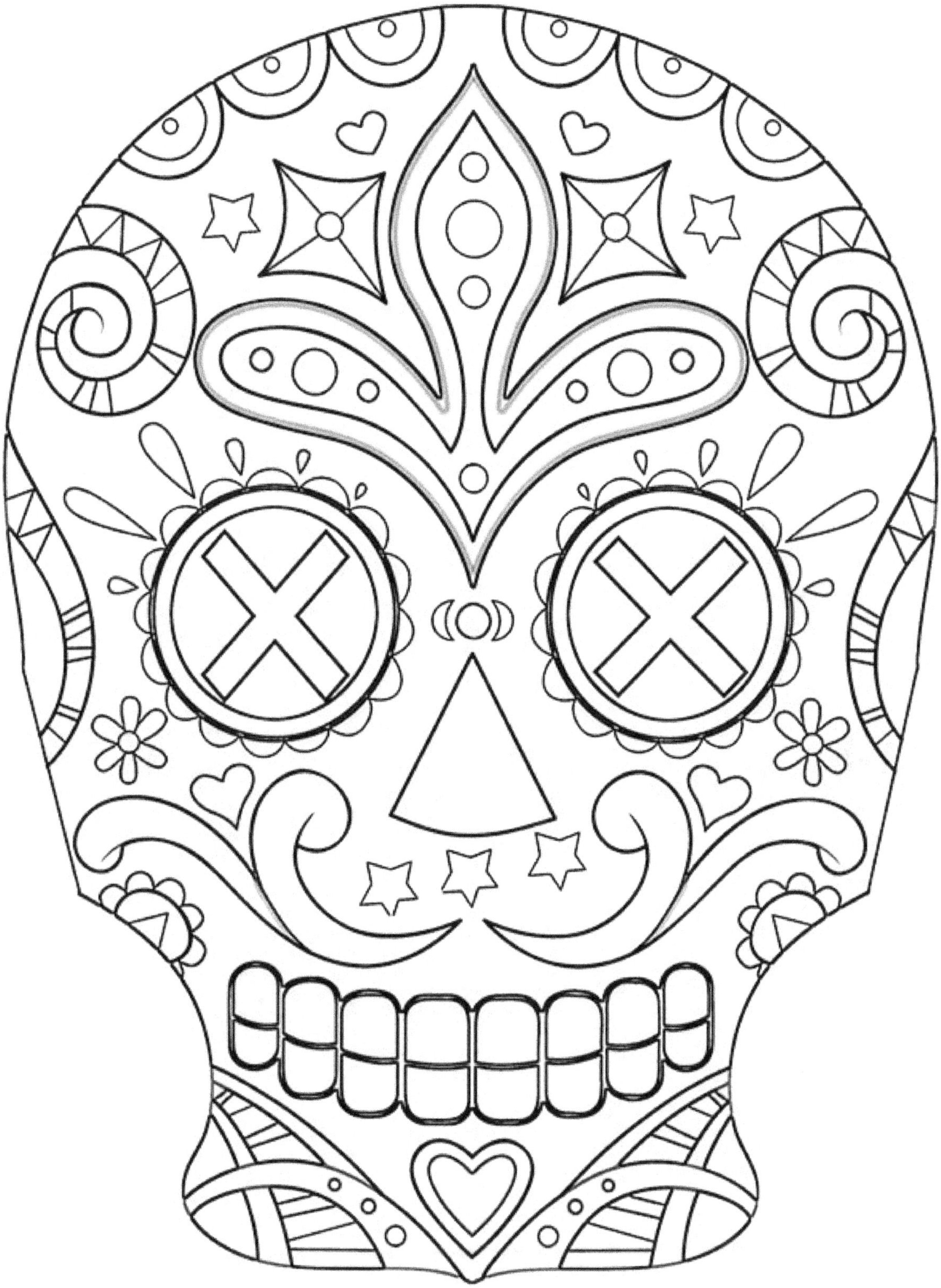

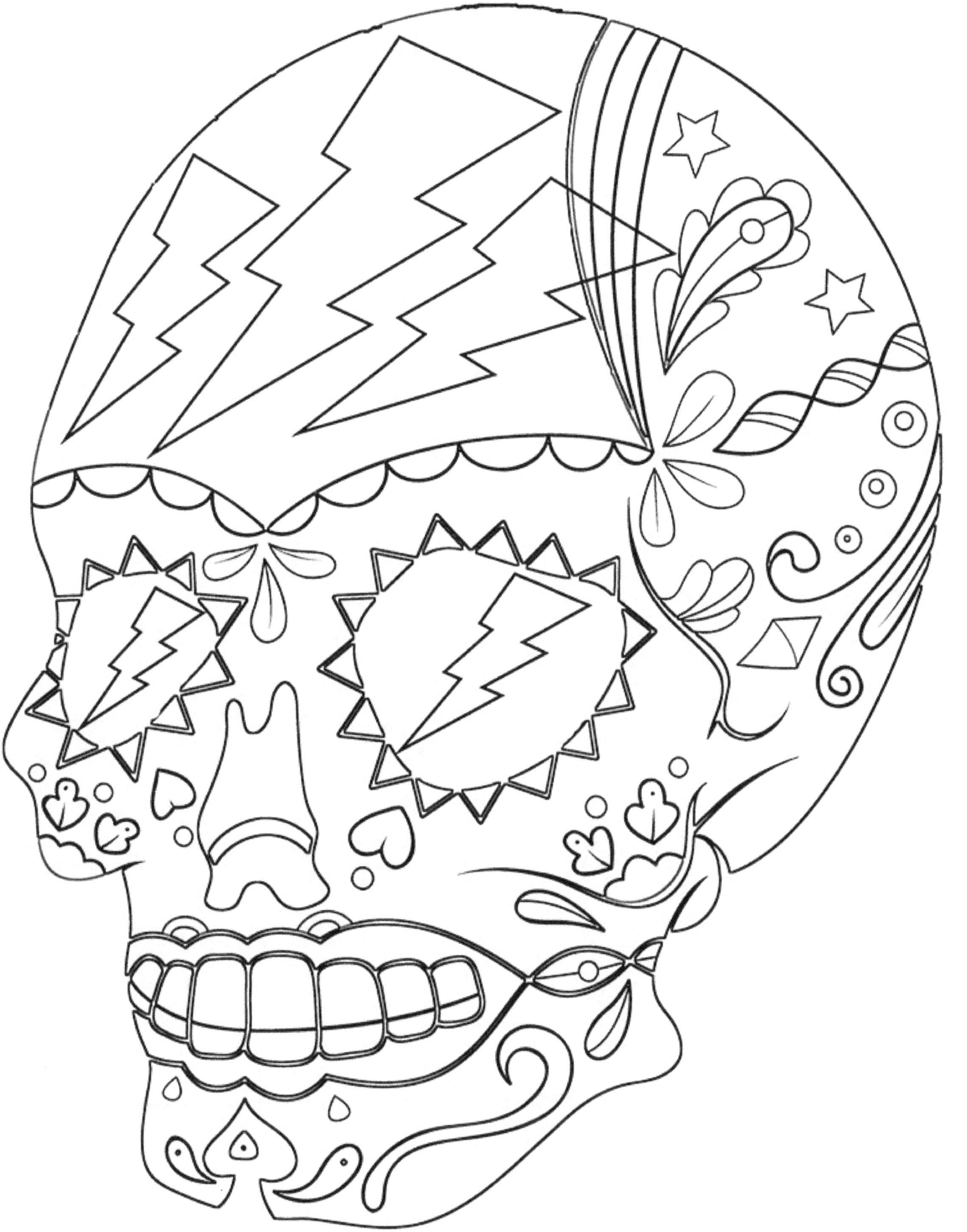

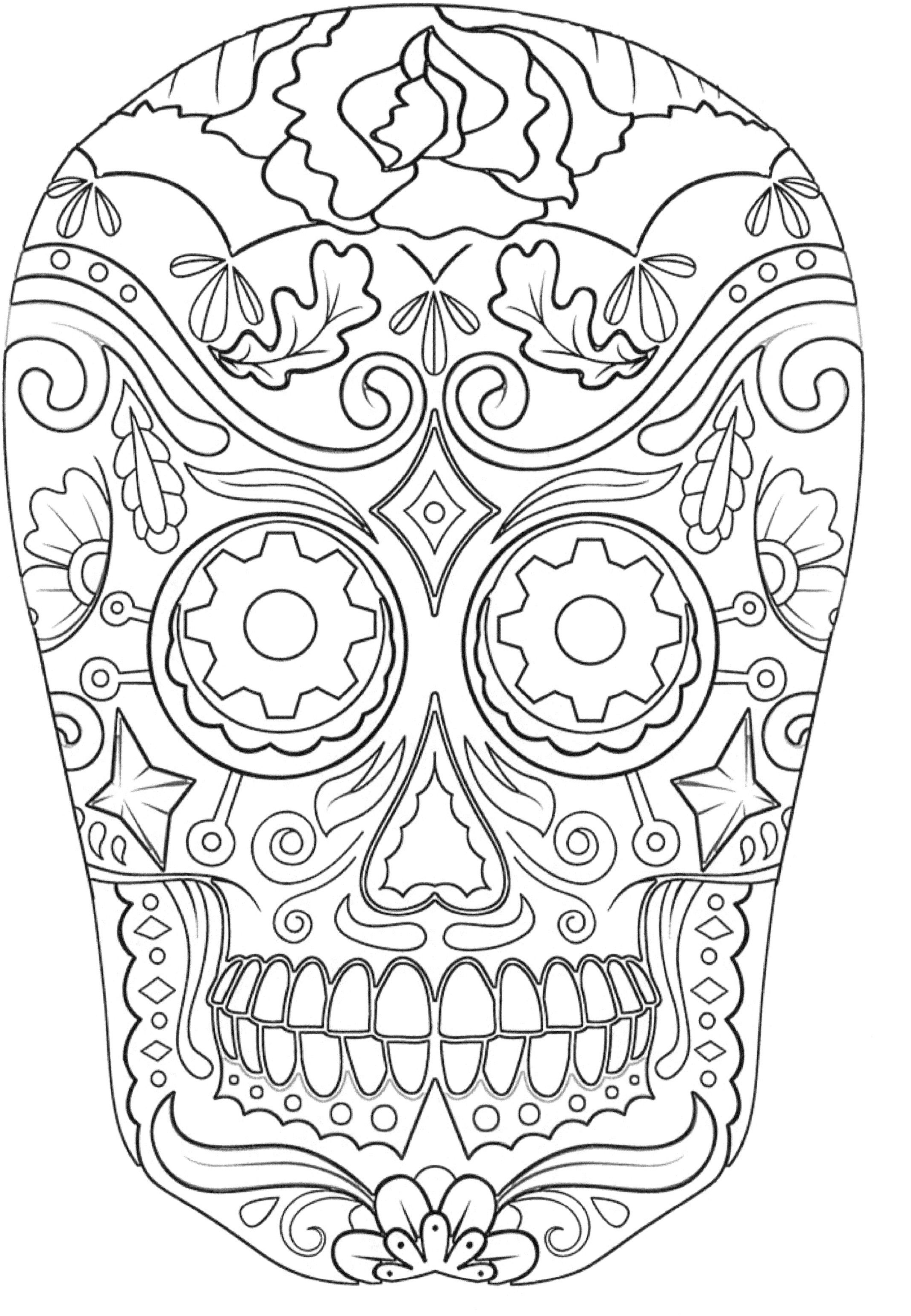

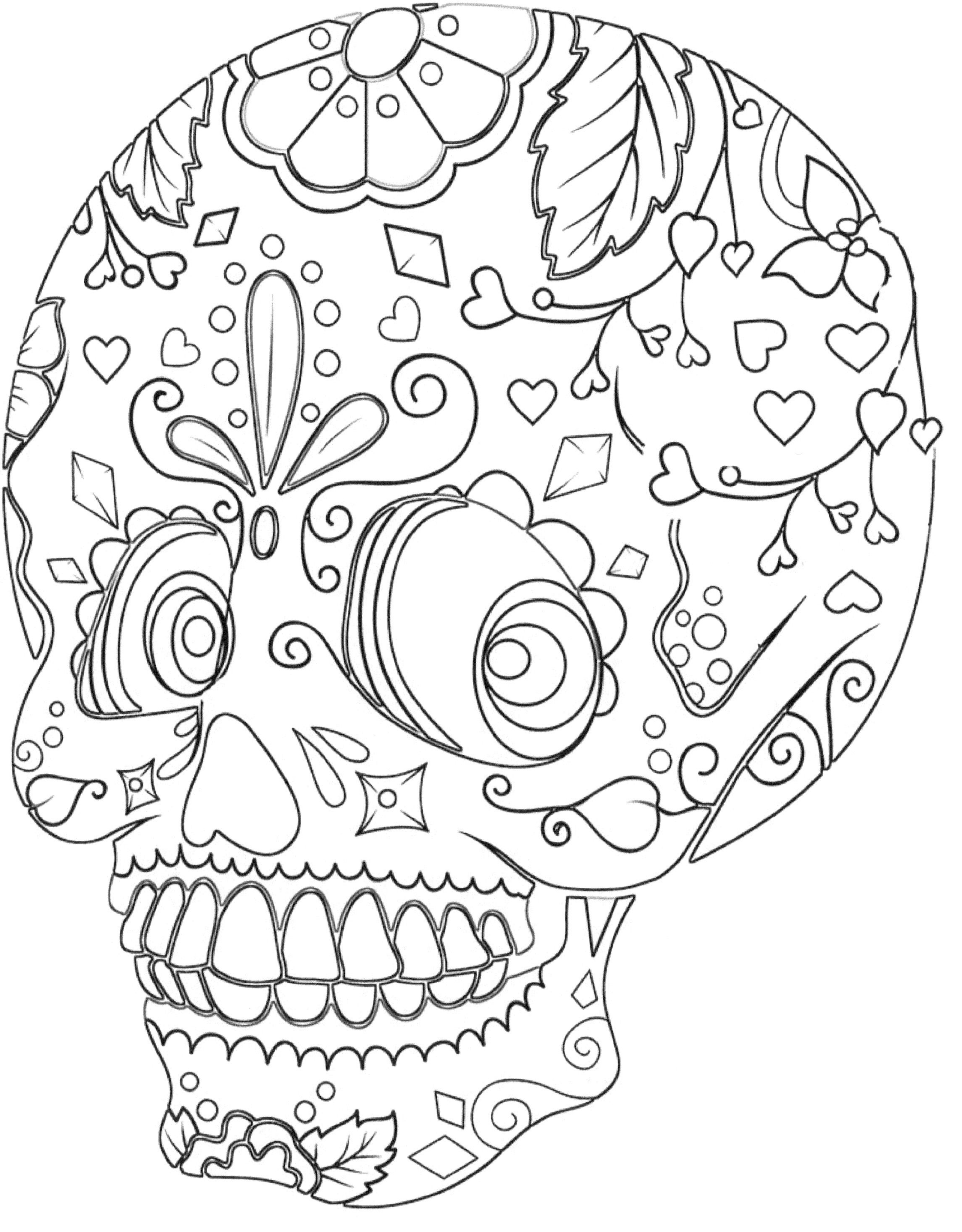

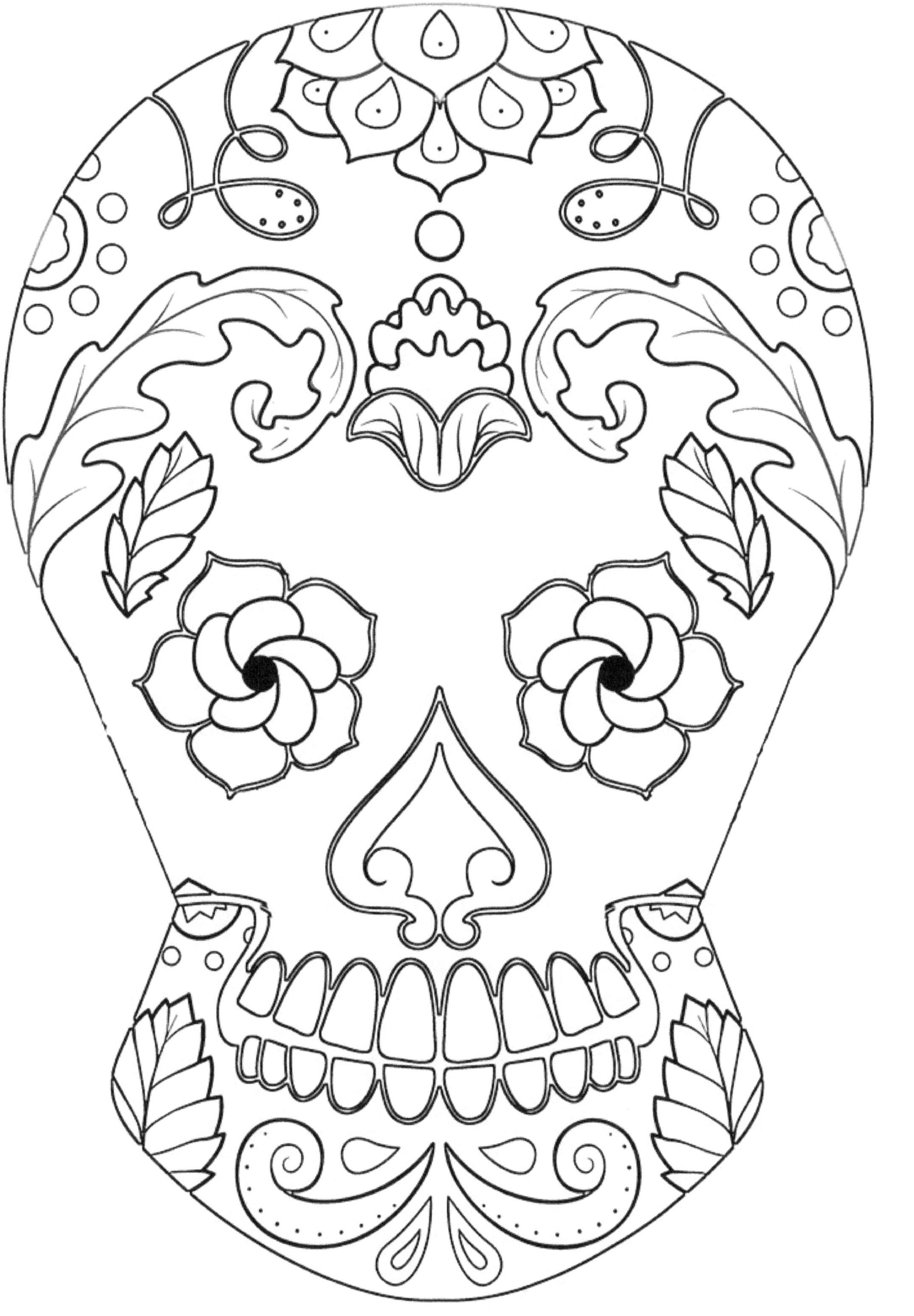

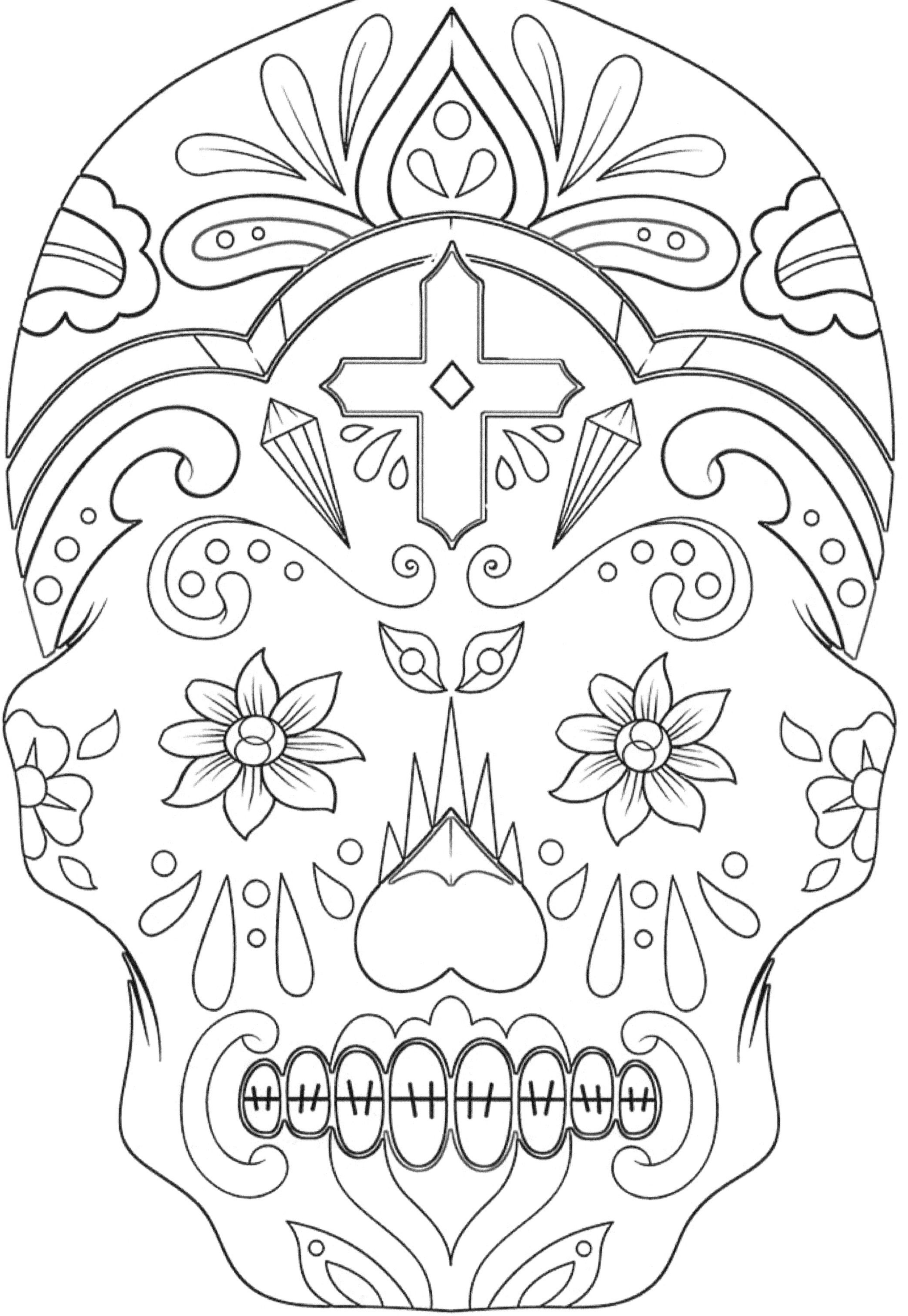

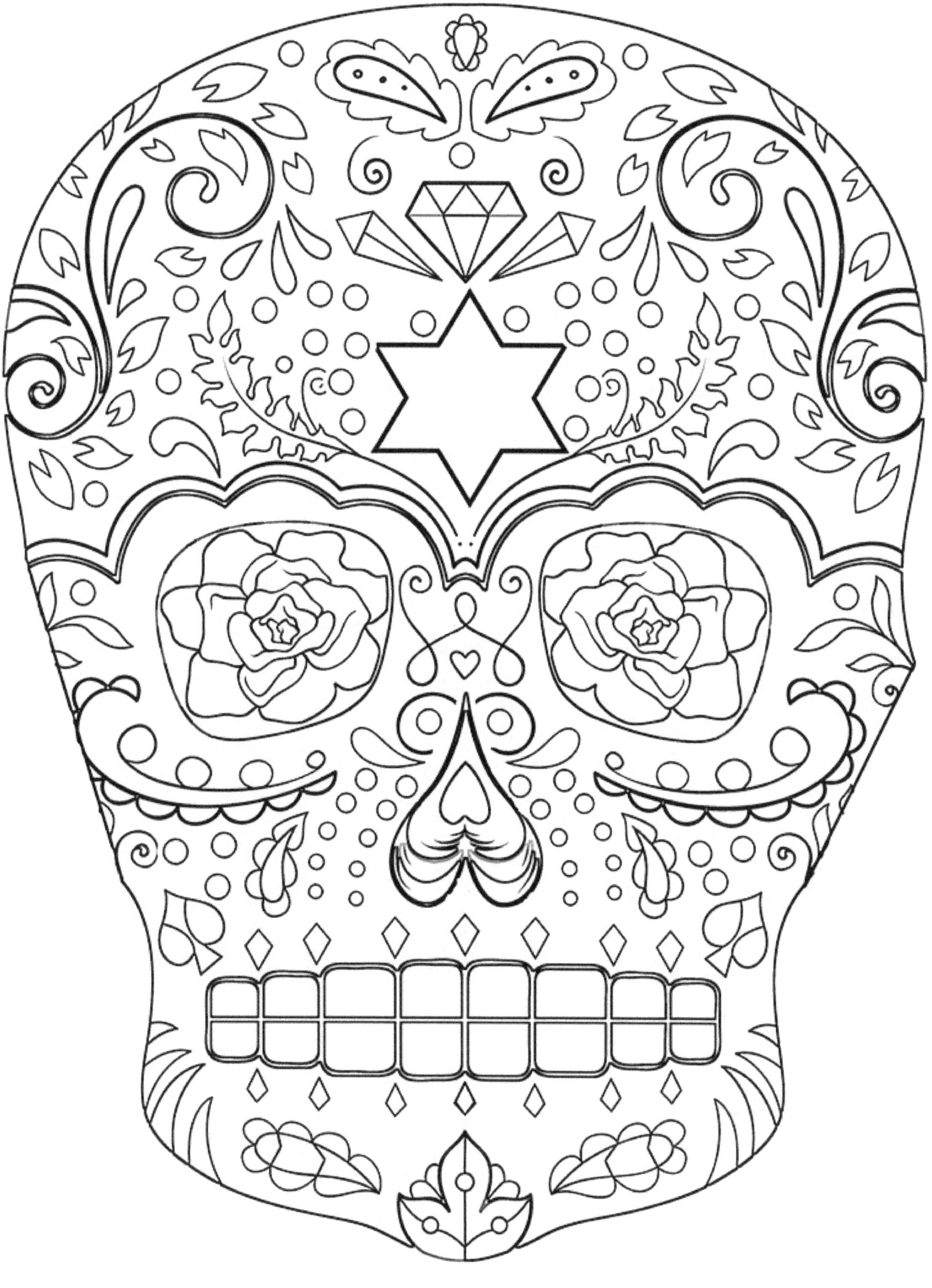

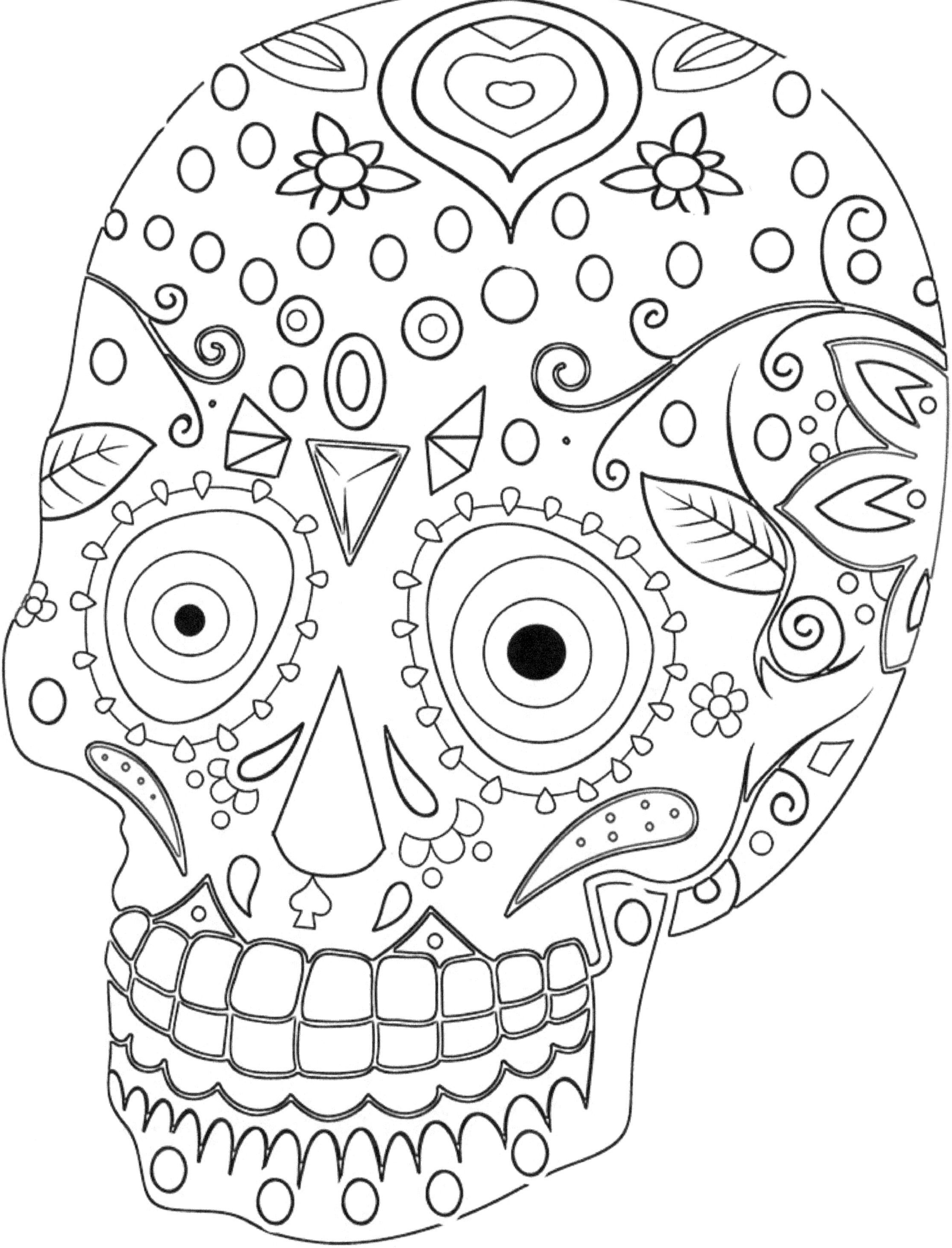

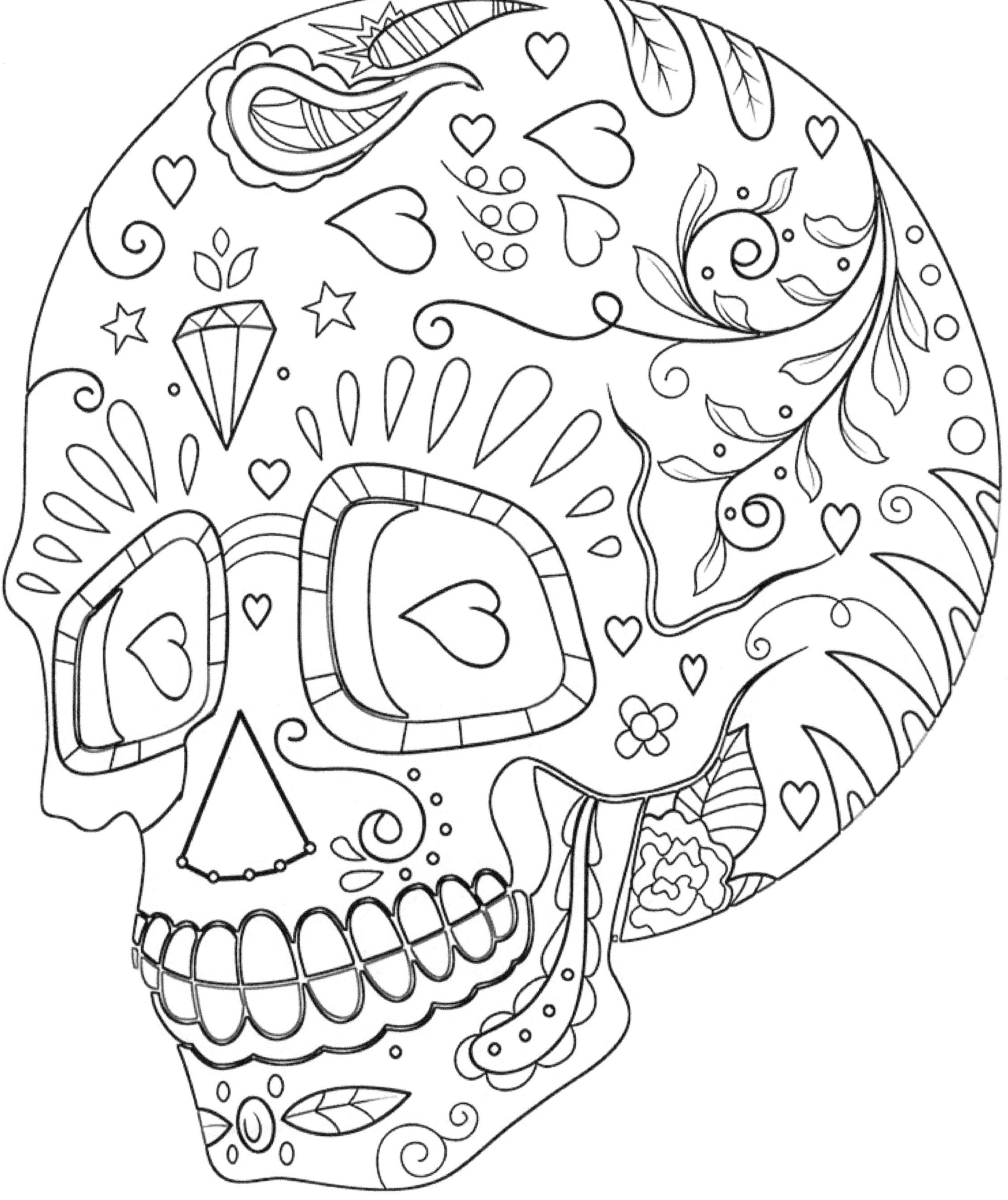

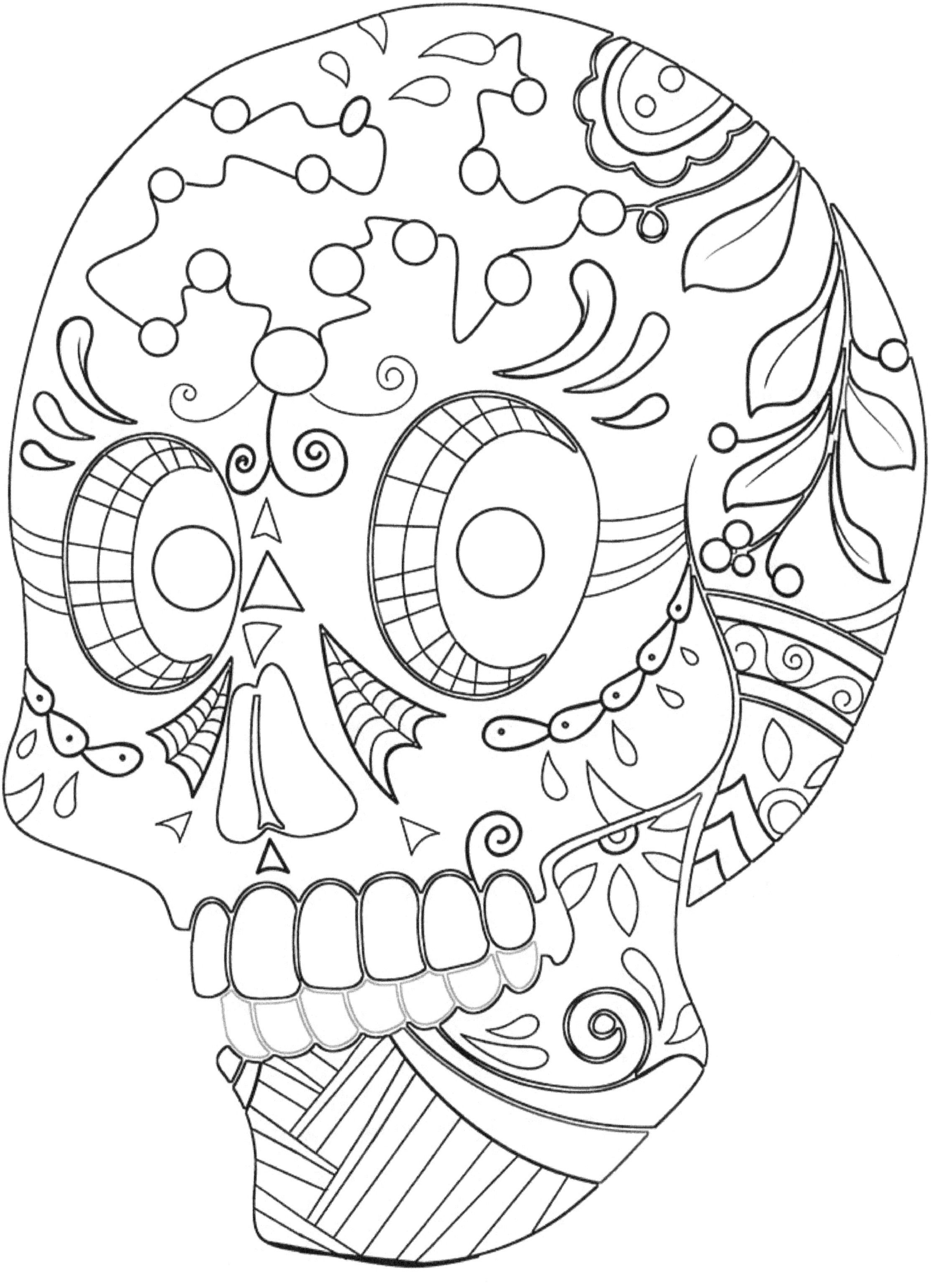

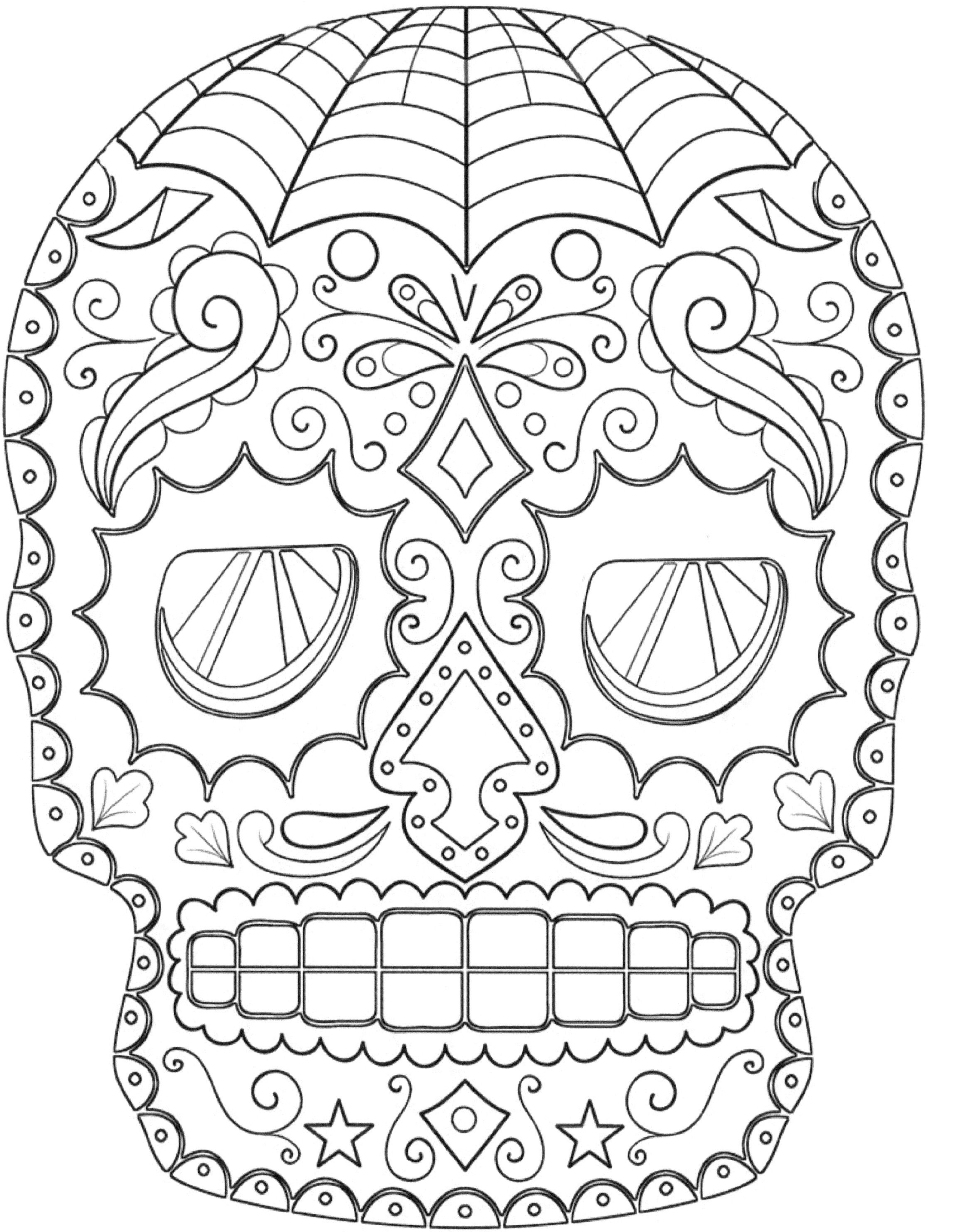

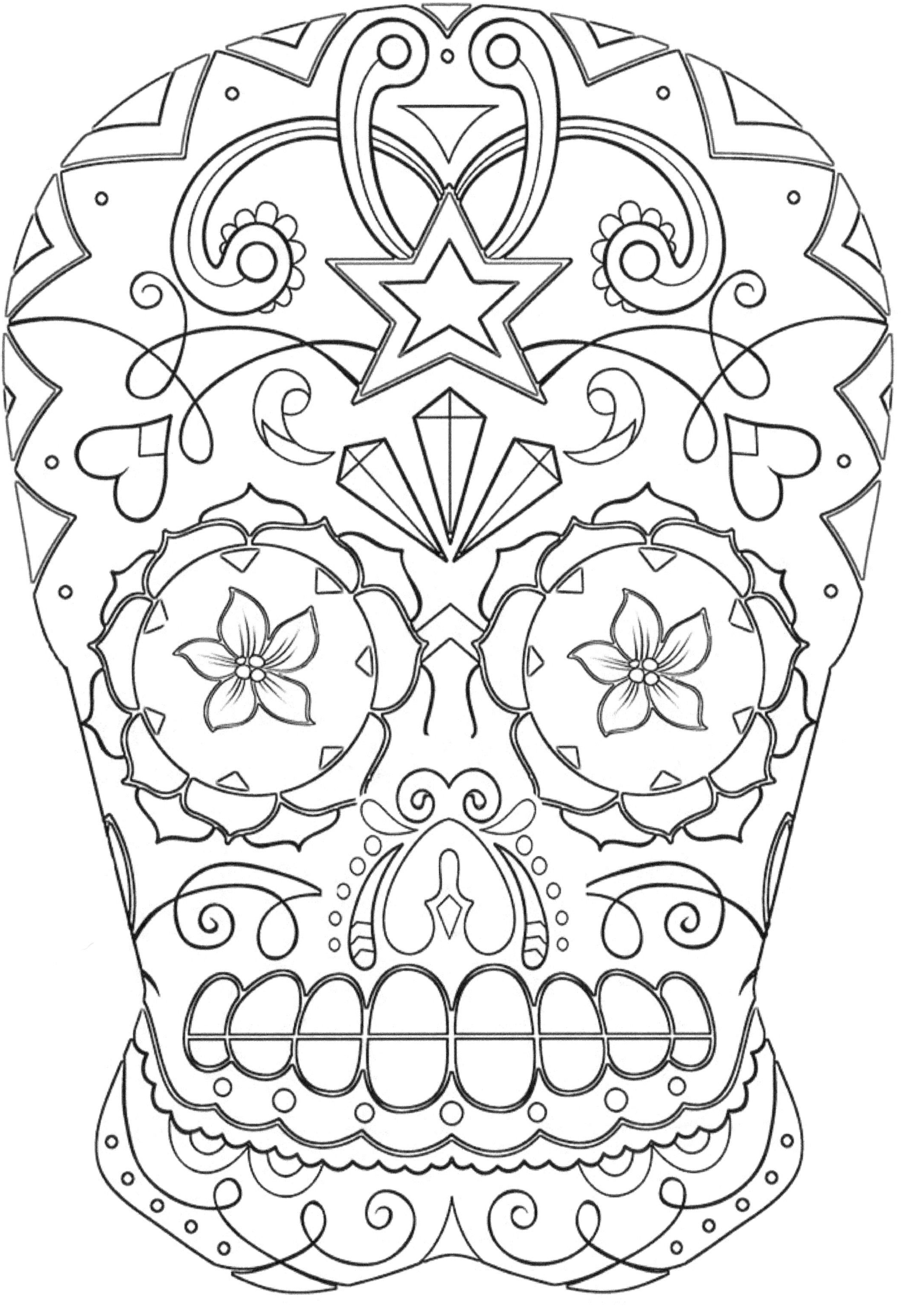

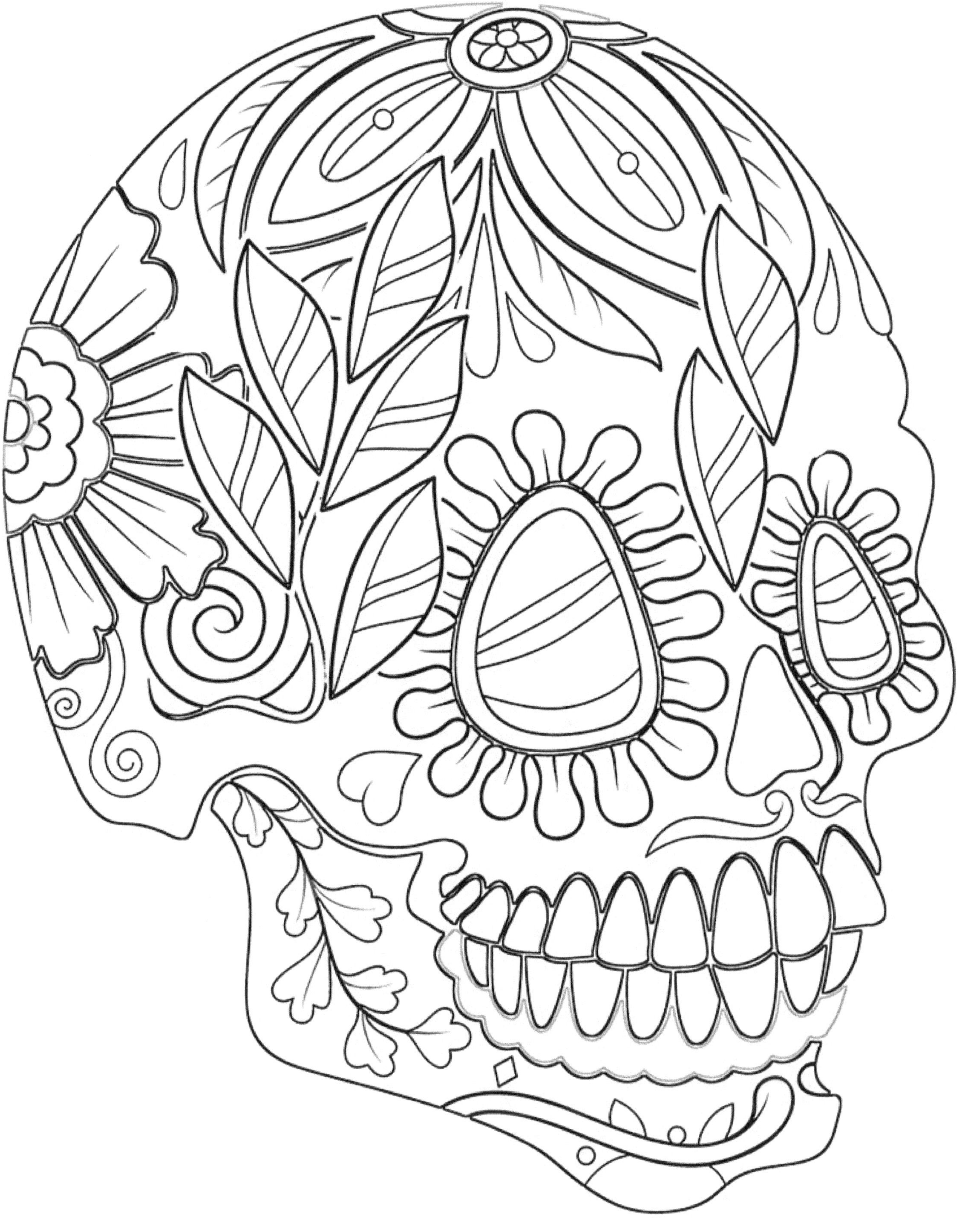

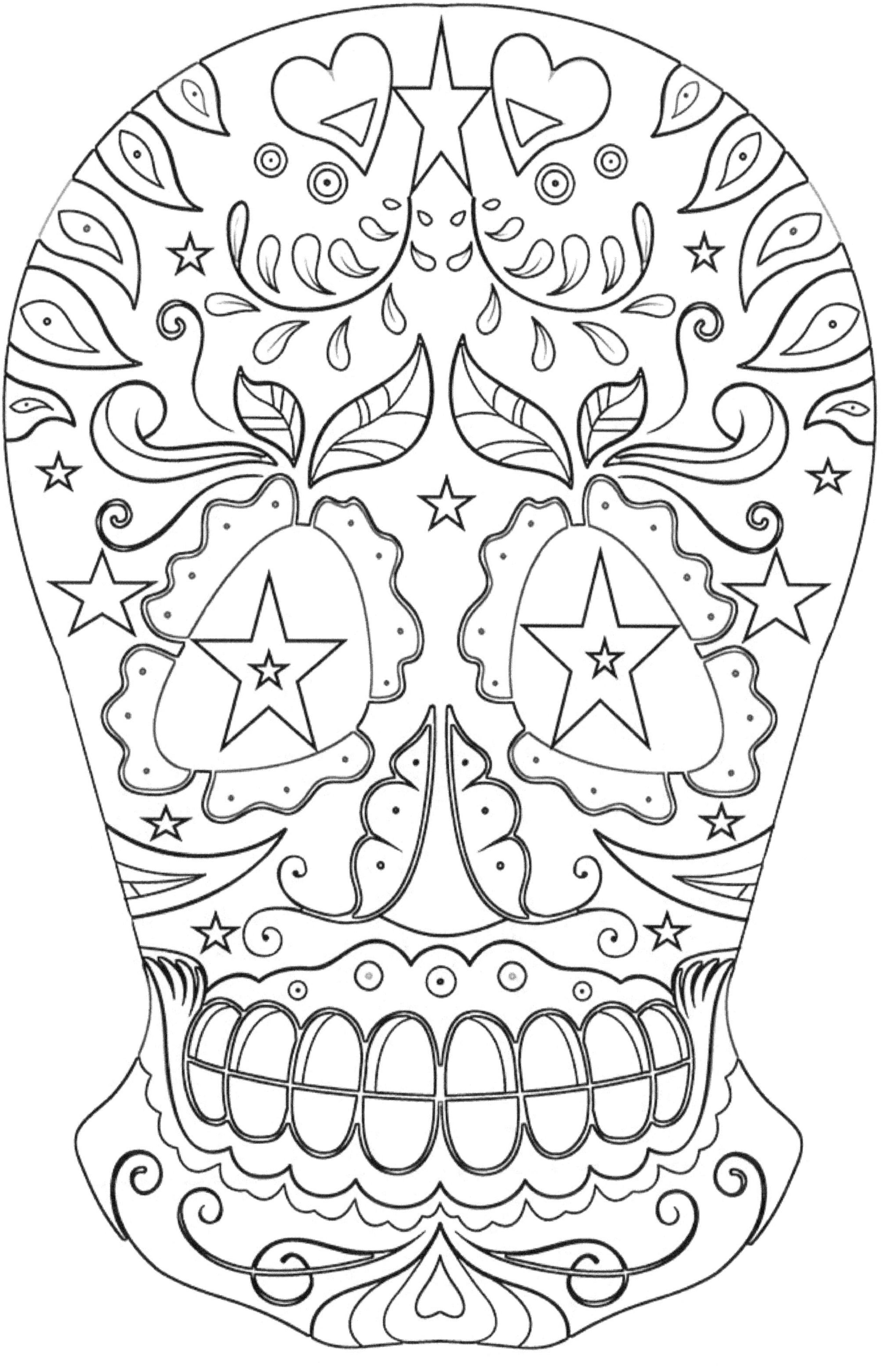

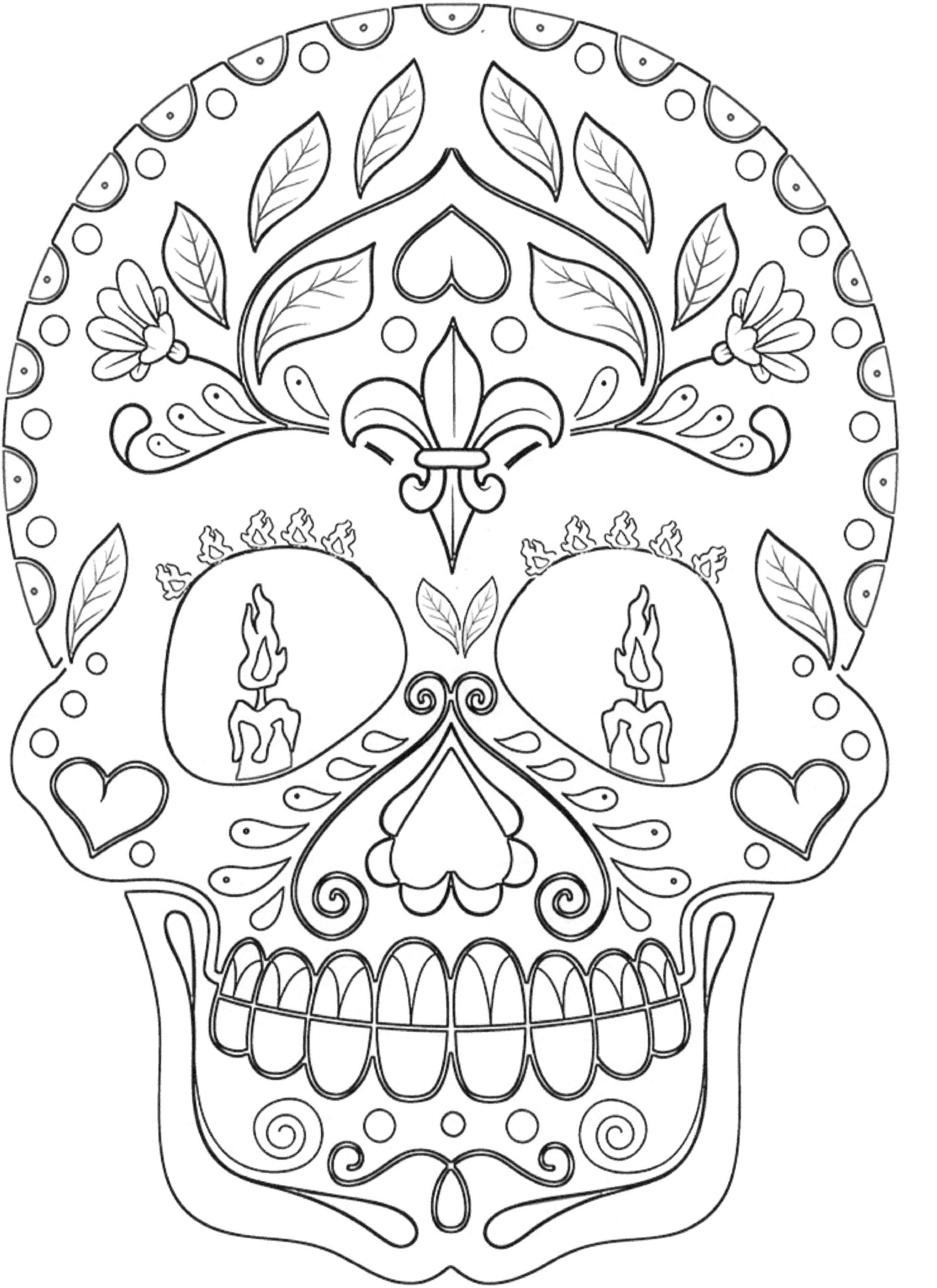

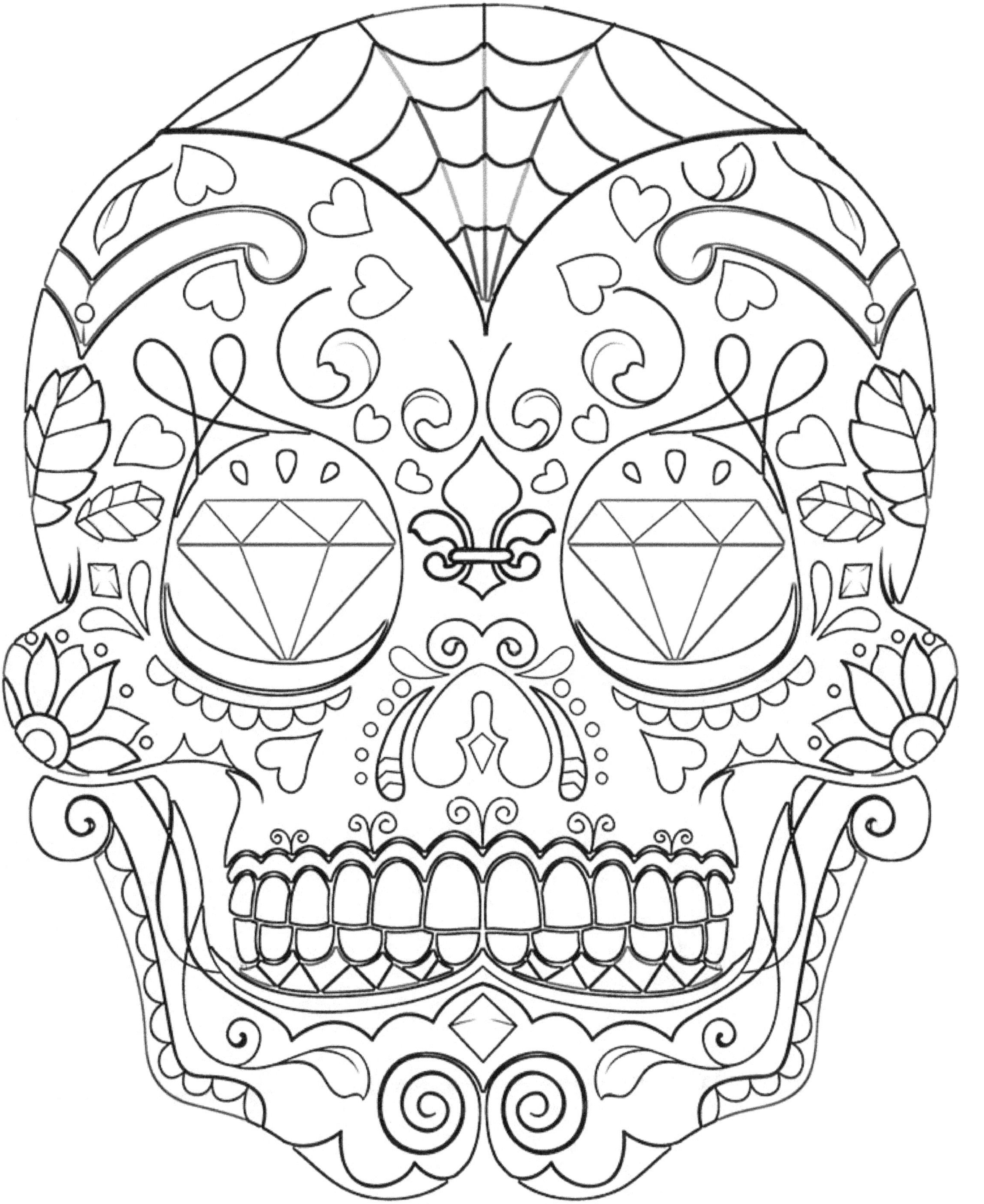

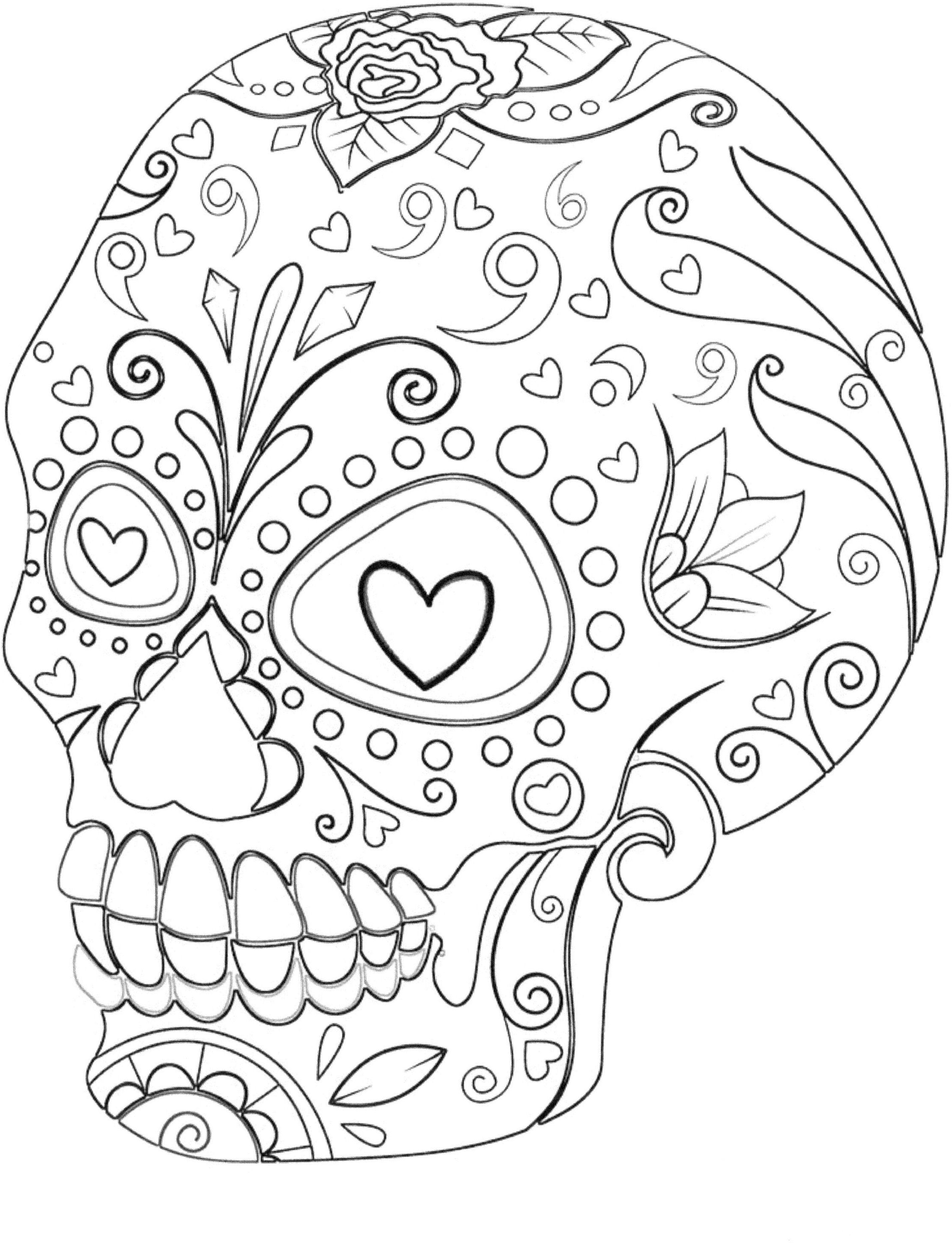

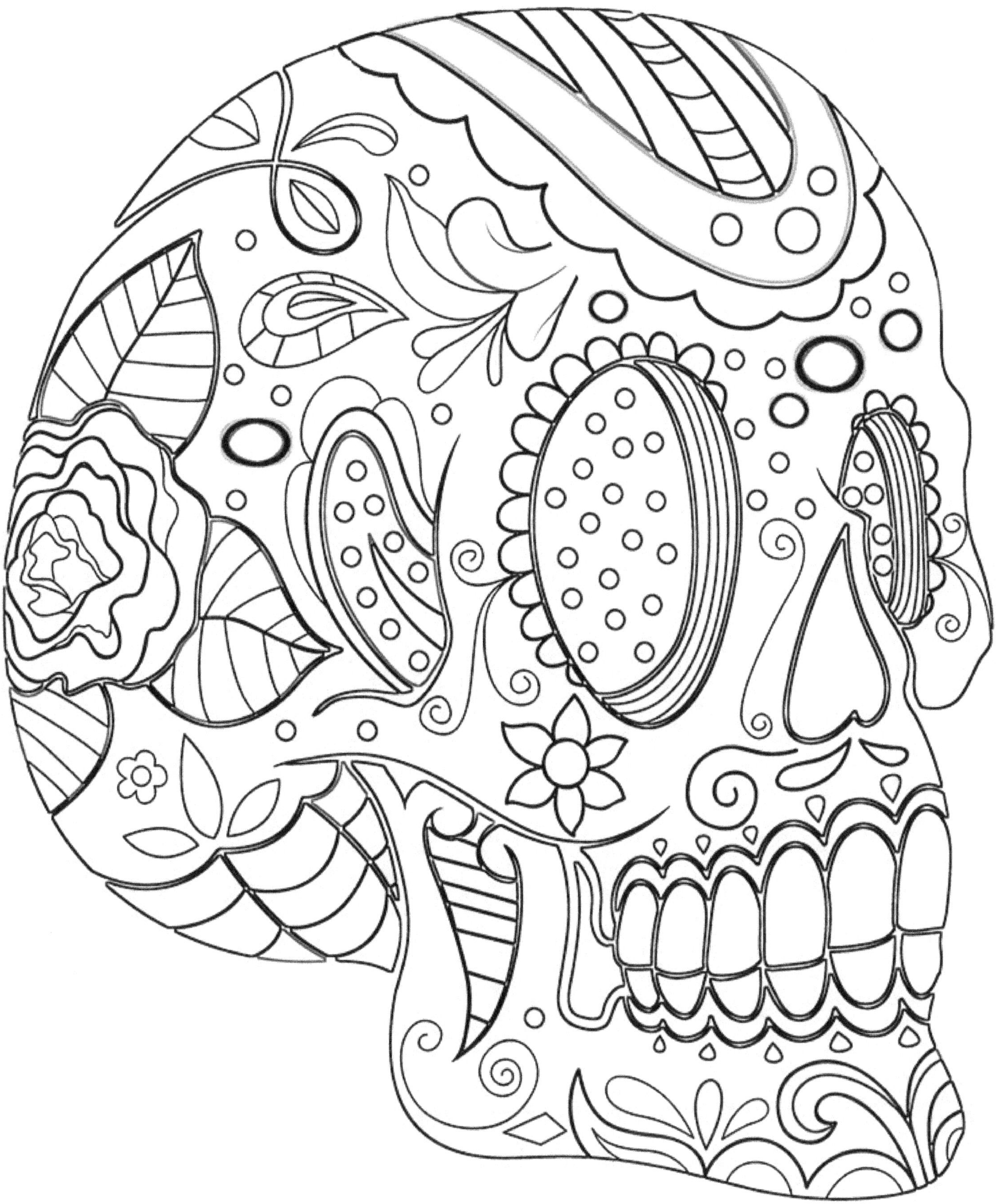

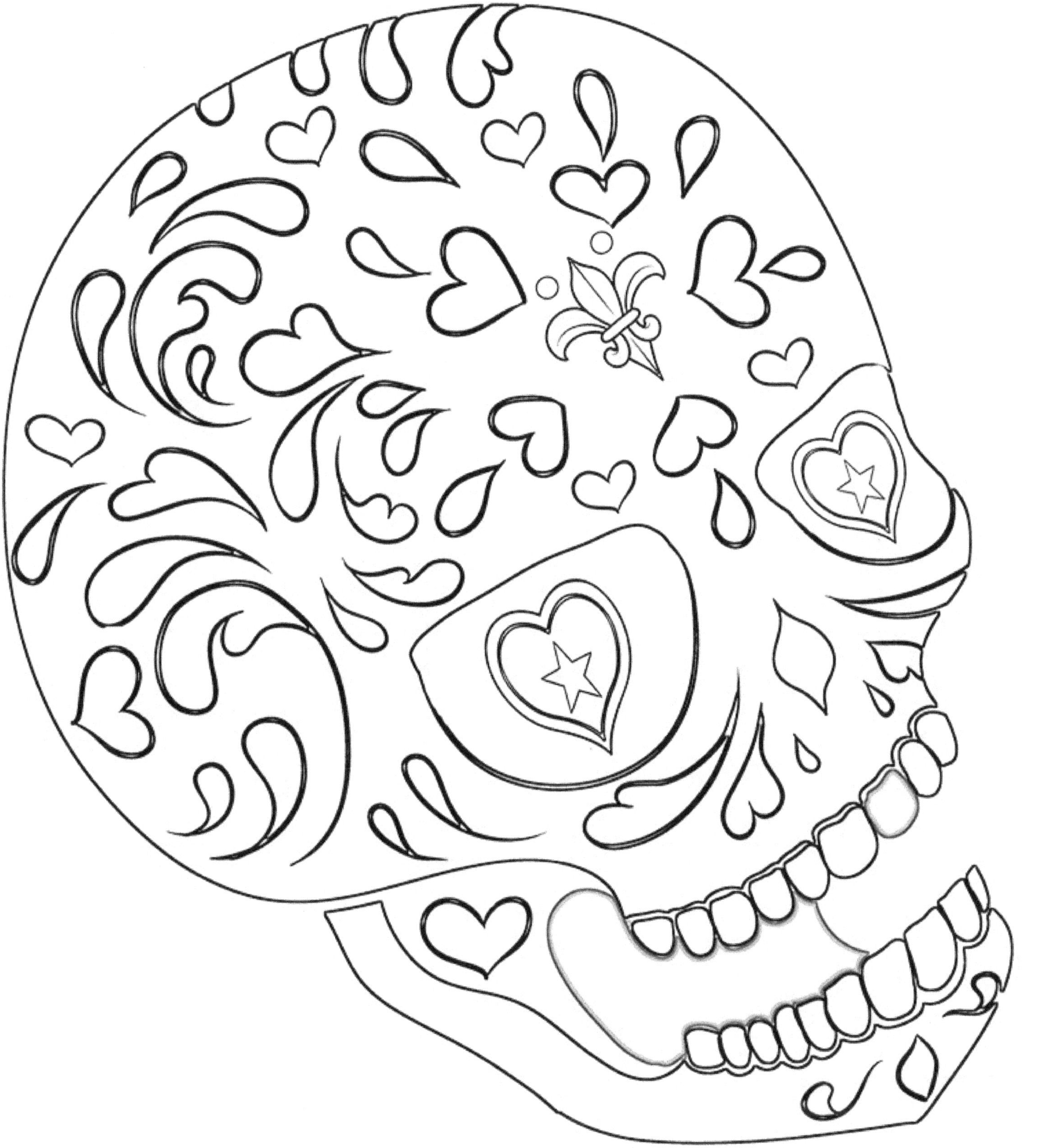

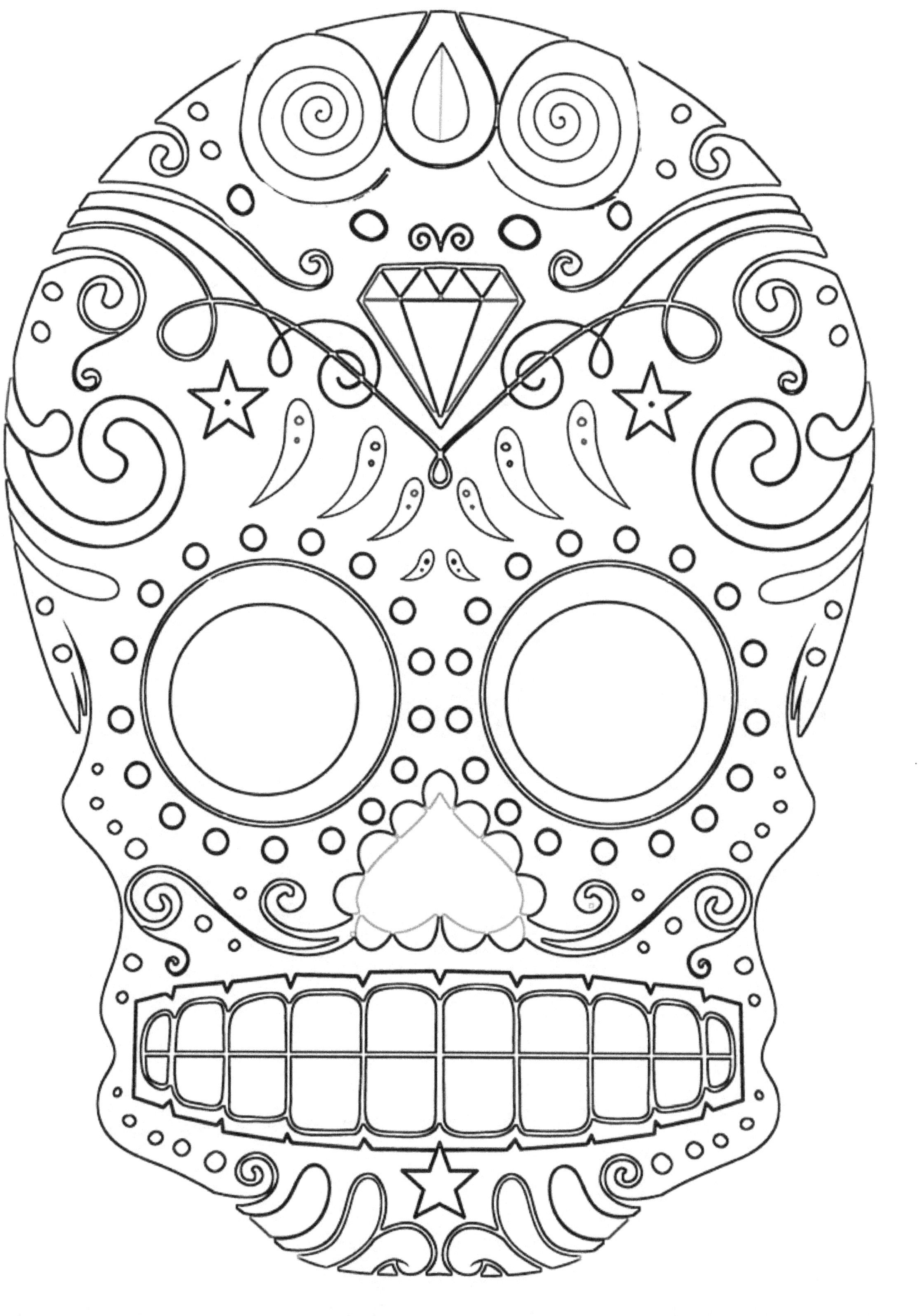

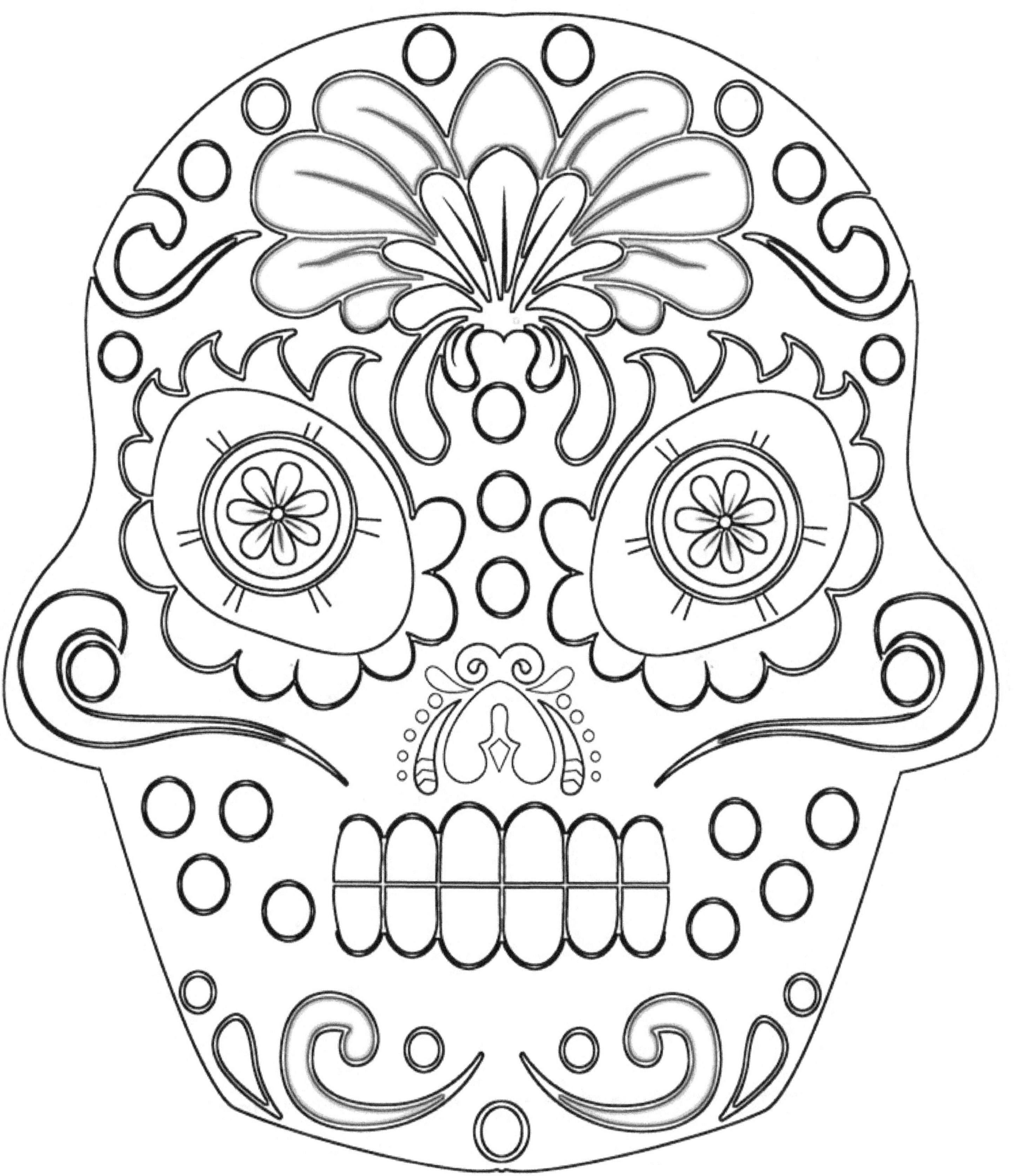

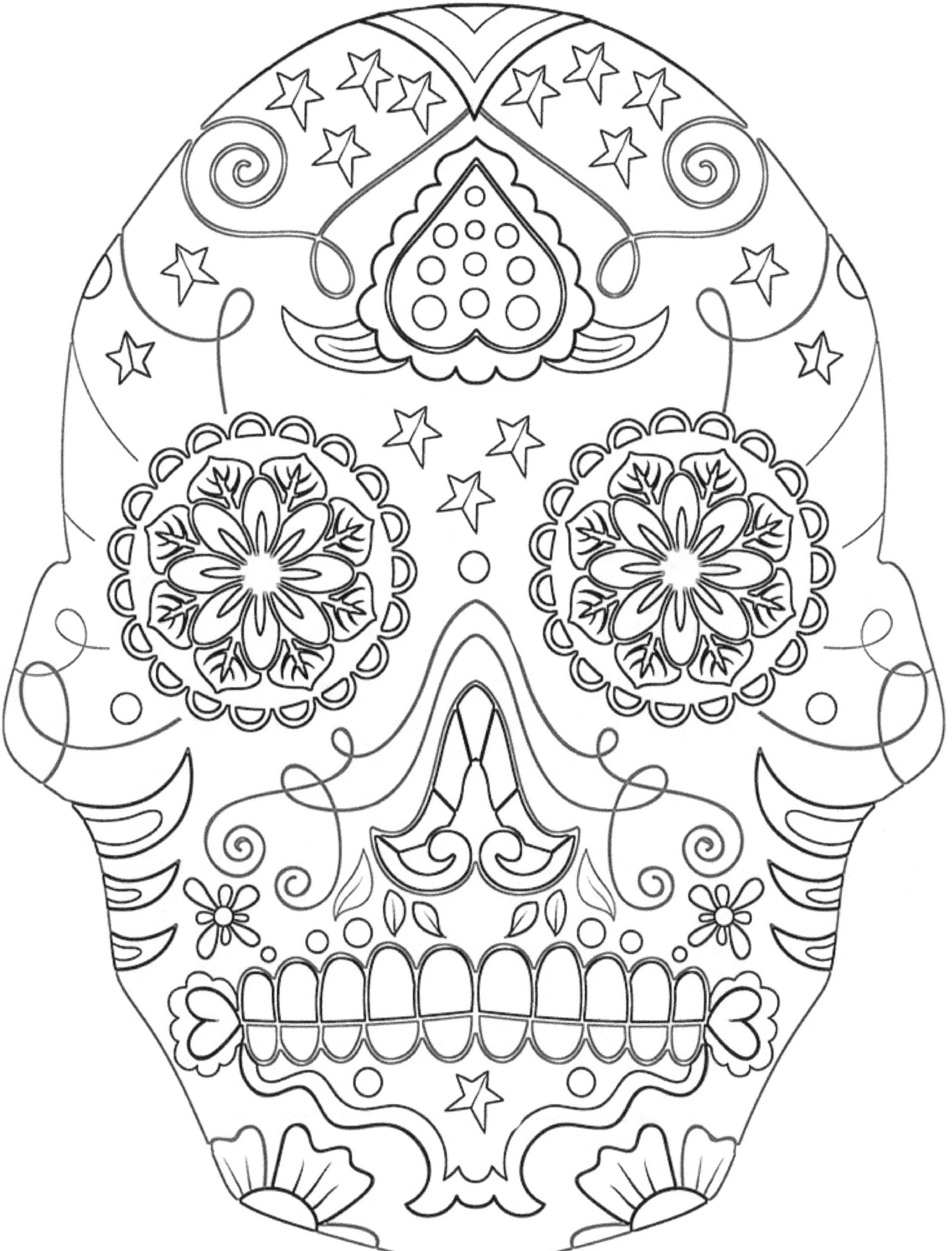

www.ingramcontent.com/pod-product-compliance
Lightning Source LLC
Chambersburg PA
CBHW081119180526
45170CB00008B/2914
* 9 7 8 1 5 2 3 3 3 7 4 3 9 *